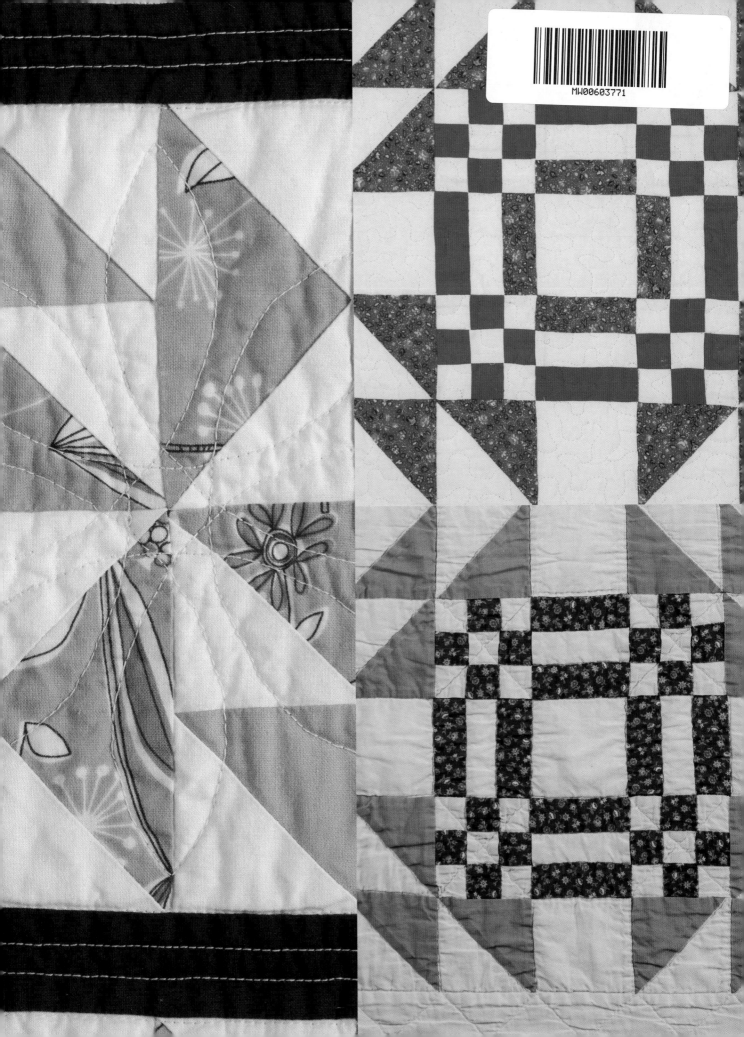

The Kansas City Stars: Best of 2013

Editors: Diane McLendon & Edie McGinnis
Designer: Kimberly Walsh
Photographer: Aaron Leimkuehler
Photo Editor: Jo Ann Groves

Published by: Kansas City Star Books
1729 Grand Boulevard
Kansas City, Mo. 64108

First edition, first printing.
ISBN:
978-1-61169-106-1

Library of Congress Control Number:
2009924512

Printed in the United States of America by Walsworth Publishing Co., Marceline, Mo.

To order copies, call toll-free 866-834-7467.

www.PickleDish.com
www.PickleDishStore.com

⭐The Kansas City Stars:
Best of 2013

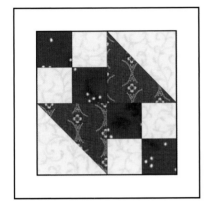
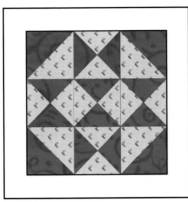
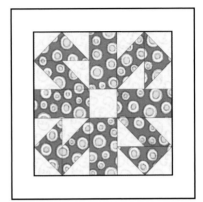
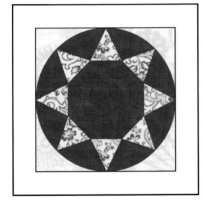
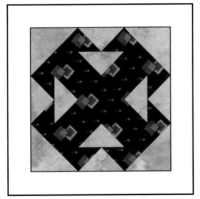

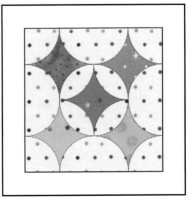

 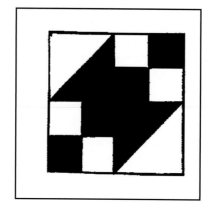 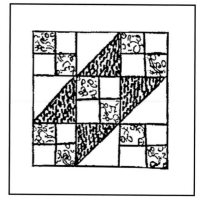

Introduction

The Kansas City Star has always appreciated tradition – from the patterns published in the newspaper in the early- to mid-1900s to the quilt books it publishes today. But what is also important is creating new traditions – and Kansas City Star Quilts embraces this as well.

A tradition that started in 2007 is our online pattern subscription called My Star Collection. Out of that grew the tradition of the My Stars series books. And out of that is this book you are holding in your hands: *The Kansas City Stars*.

This book includes 25 of our favorite patterns that were published via My Star Collection in 2013. These patterns are special – they are redrafted, updated patterns that were published in the newspaper between 1928 and 1961. You will find many of your favorite "oldies but goodies," such as Jacob's Ladder, King's Crown, and Cherry Basket. You may also discover some new patterns to love, such as Buckeye Beauty, Jinx Star, and Gretchen.

Included with these patterns is a real treat – actual quilts made up in these patterns from fans just like you! The patterns also include the original sketch and caption of the pattern that was printed in the newspaper those many years ago.

So sit back and enjoy this new tradition while remembering the importance of keeping old traditions alive.

About the Historical Patterns

The Kansas City Star newspaper began printing traditional quilt patterns in 1928. The patterns were a weekly feature in The Star or its sister publications, *The Weekly Star* and the *Star Farmer*, from 1928 until the mid-1930s, then less regularly until 1961. By the time the last one ran, more than 1,000 had been published in the papers, which circulated in seven Midwestern states as well as North Carolina, Kentucky, and Texas.

About My Star Collection

My Star Collection is a weekly subscription service where subscribers download a pdf pattern – from The Kansas City Star's historical 1928 to 1961 collection – each week. The patterns include updated fabric requirements, templates, rotary cutting instructions, and assembly instructions. To date, we've republished more than 300 of these traditional patterns. The subscription includes a year of patterns – 52 in all – for only $20. For more information or to sign up, visit subscriptions.pickledish.com.

Acknowledgements

I would like to thank the wonderful team that has made this book and My Star Collection possible: Edie McGinnis, Kim Walsh, Jane Miller, Doug Weaver, Aaron Leimkuehler, Jo Ann Groves, Deb Bauer, Deb Rowden, and of course, our quilt friends who have graciously provided their quilts to be included in this book.

Diane McLendon
Editor

TABLE OF CONTENTS

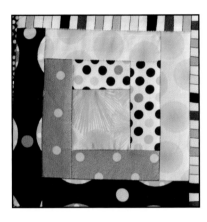

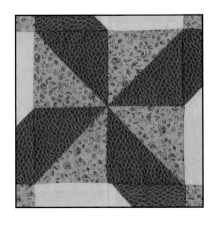

Dutchman's Puzzle

Appeared in The Star **March 29, 1930**

12" finished block

Fabric Needed
Cream
Blue print
Navy blue

Cutting Instructions

From the cream colored fabric, cut
8 – 3 7/8" squares. Cut the squares from corner to corner once on the diagonal or cut 16 triangles using template A.

From the blue print fabric, cut
1 – 7 1/4" square. Cut the square from corner to corner twice on the diagonal or cut 4 triangles using template B.

From the navy blue fabric, cut
1 – 7 1/4" square. Cut the square from corner to corner twice on the diagonal or cut 4 triangles.

To Make the Block

Sew a cream A triangle to either side of a blue print B triangle. Make 4 of these flying geese units.

Sew a cream A triangle to either side of a navy blue B triangle. Make 4 of these flying geese units.

Sew the flying geese units into sets of 2. This makes one quadrant of the block. Make 4.

Sew the four quadrants together to complete the block.

The Kansas City Stars:
Best of 2013

Dutchman's Puzzle Templates

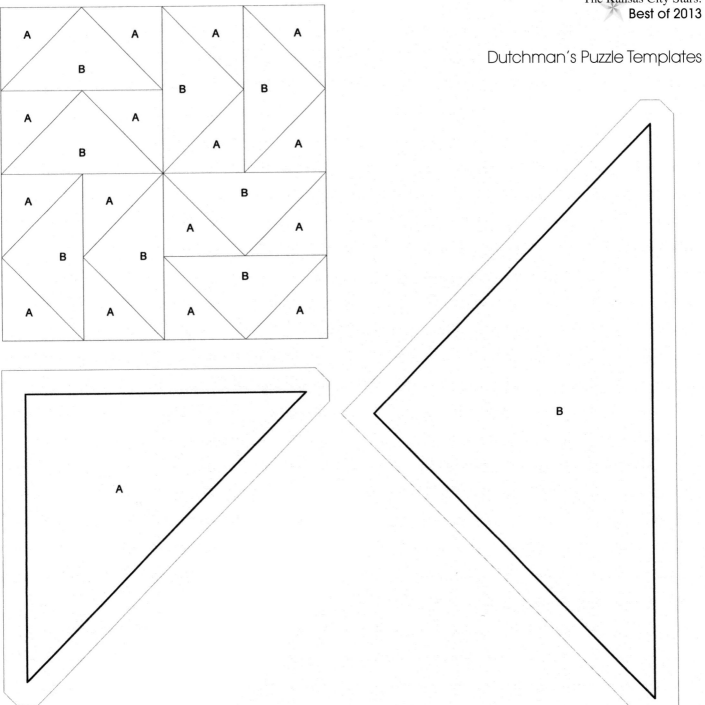

From The Kansas City Star, March 29, 1930: Number 90
Original Size - 12"

This is a "double-header" number in The Star quilt series with no additional charge for admission! In two clever ways it proves what can be done with a pair of triangles, one half the area of the other. In "Dutchman's Puzzle" two smaller triangles add to a larger about like the cutting chart patterns are placed and this twice done forms a square, one-fourth of the finished block. The darker always points into the lighter and thus the puzzle is solved in a 12-inch block. "Windmill" is quite a different arrangement, even more simple, which makes a block eight and one-half inches square.

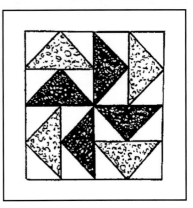

"Dutchman's Puzzle," designed, pieced, and quilted by Peggy Dodge, Kansas City, Mo.

Cherry Basket

Appeared in The Star **October 24, 1928**

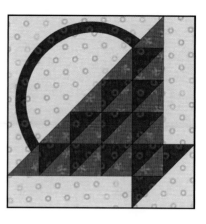

12" finished block

Fabric Needed
Tan
Brown
Pink

Cutting Instructions

From the tan, cut

1 – 10 7/8" square. Cut the square from corner to corner once on the diagonal. There is no template given for this piece due to page constraints. (You will have one triangle left over.)

2 – 2 1/2" x 8 1/2" rectangles or use template B.

1 – 4 7/8" square. Cut the square from corner to corner once on the diagonal or use template C. (You will have one triangle left over.)

From the brown fabric, cut

1 handle using template E.

6 – 2 7/8" squares. Cut each square from corner to corner once on the diagonal or cut 12 triangles using template D.

From the pink, cut

8 – 2 7/8" squares. Cut each square from corner to corner once on the diagonal or cut 16 triangles using template D. (You will have one triangle left over.)

To Make the Block

Sew a tan B rectangle to a brown D triangle. Make 2. One must mirror the other. See the illustration below. Set aside.

Sew the pink D triangles to the brown D triangles into rows as shown.

Sew the rows together and add the B/D units.

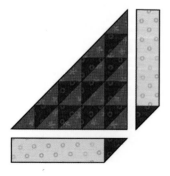

Cherry Basket Templates

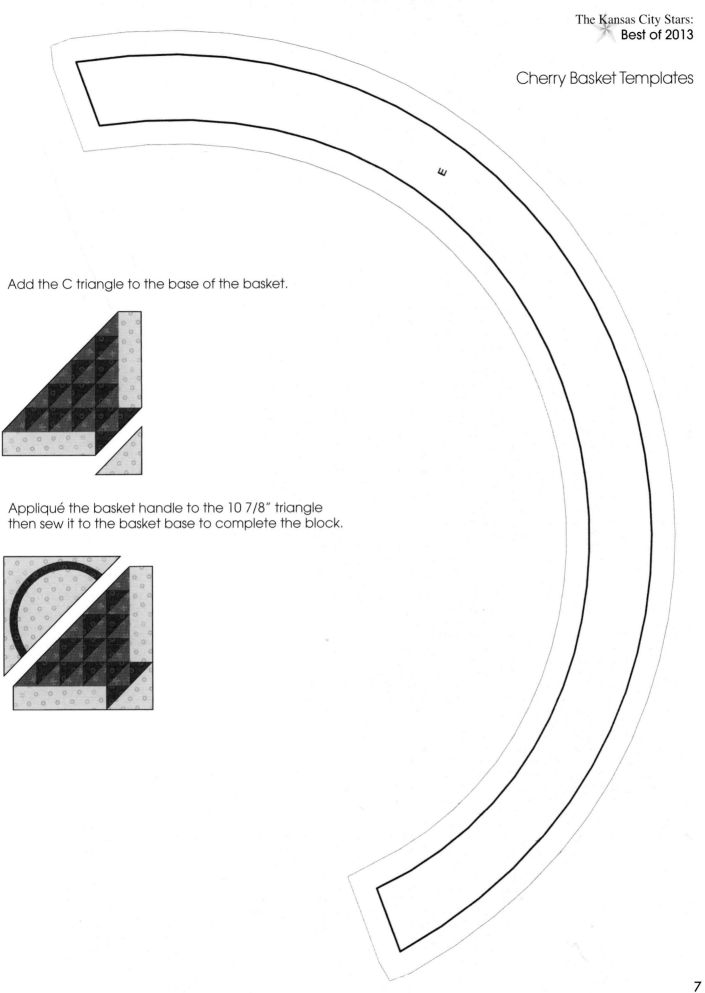

E

Add the C triangle to the base of the basket.

Appliqué the basket handle to the 10 7/8" triangle
then sew it to the basket base to complete the block.

"Cherry Basket," owned by Edie McGinnis, Kansas City, Mo.

From The Kansas City Star, October 24, 1928: No. 6
Original size – 12"

The cherry basket pattern is excellent for a patchwork pillow as well as for colonial quilts. The following colors are suggested for it - brown printed material for the basket and handle, red print for the "cherries" (the red triangles which alternate with the brown triangles in the basket) and unbleached muslin for the background. One block is twelve inches square when complete. Patterns for all parts are given here except for the large triangle for the top half of the square upon which the handle is appliqued. This triangle is easily made, for it measures exactly ten inches on the two sides. To make a pattern for it, fold a piece of paper in half to form a right angle. Then measure down ten inches on each side and draw across for the base of the triangle and cut, allowing for seams. Rememebr these patterns do not allow for seams. Trace them on cardboard, then cut out the cardboard patterns. Place the cardboard patterns on the material, draw around them with a pencil and then cut outside the pencil line to allow for a seam, but sew on the pencil line. Piece the red and brown, triangles together, following the pattern at the upper left. It sets together always with alternating squares on the diagonal. The unbleached material fills in the four sides as shown.

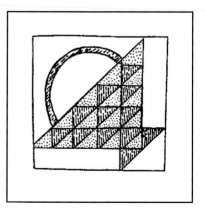

Cherry Basket Templates

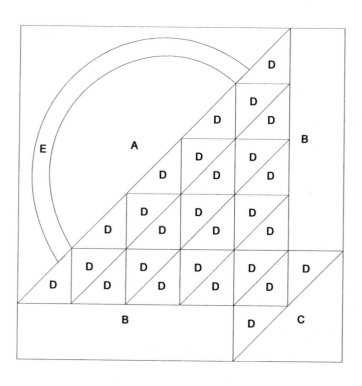

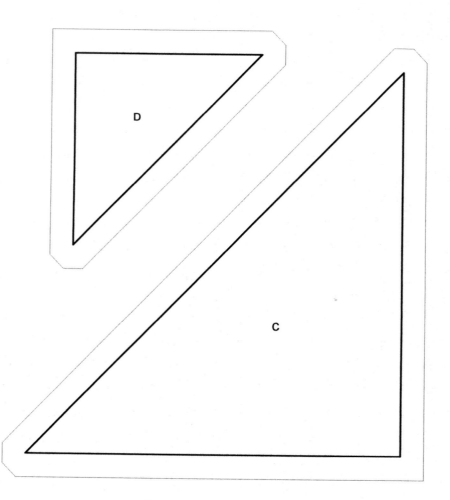

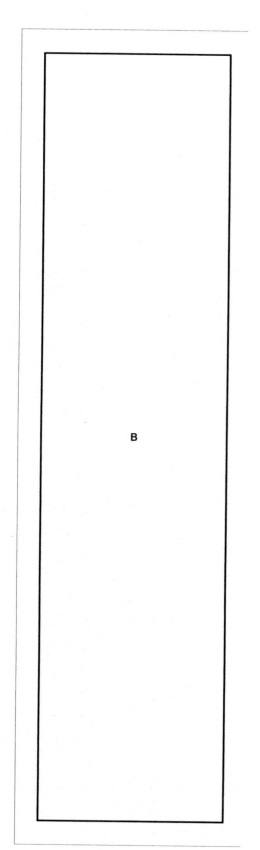

"Cherry Basket," owned by Edie McGinnis, Kansas City, Mo. Maker and quilter unknown.

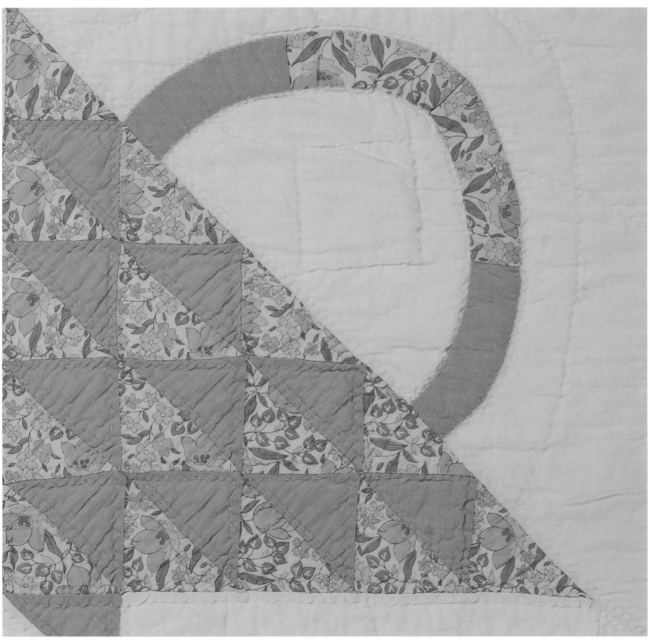

Jinx Star

Appeared in The Star **April 14, 1934**

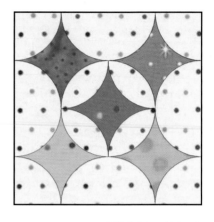

Cutting Instructions

From each of the colored pieces, cut
1 piece using template A. Add 1/8″ – 1/4″ seam allowance when cutting.

From the background fabric, cut
1 – 12 1/2″ square.

12" finished block

Fabric Needed
Dark blue
Purple
Yellow
Dark pink
Light blue
Background
(I used small polka dots.)

To Make the Block

Fold the background fabric from corner to corner twice on the diagonal and lightly press the folds in place. The folds will help you place the pieces correctly.

Prepare the pieces for appliqué using your favorite method.

Refer to the diagram and pin the pieces to the background square and stitch in place.

Jinx Star Template

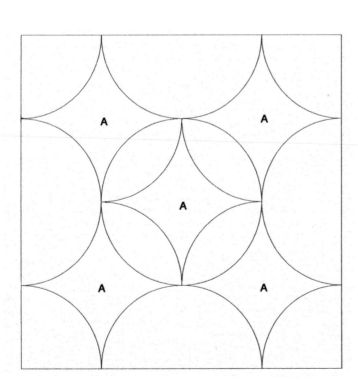

The Kansas City Stars:
Best of 2013

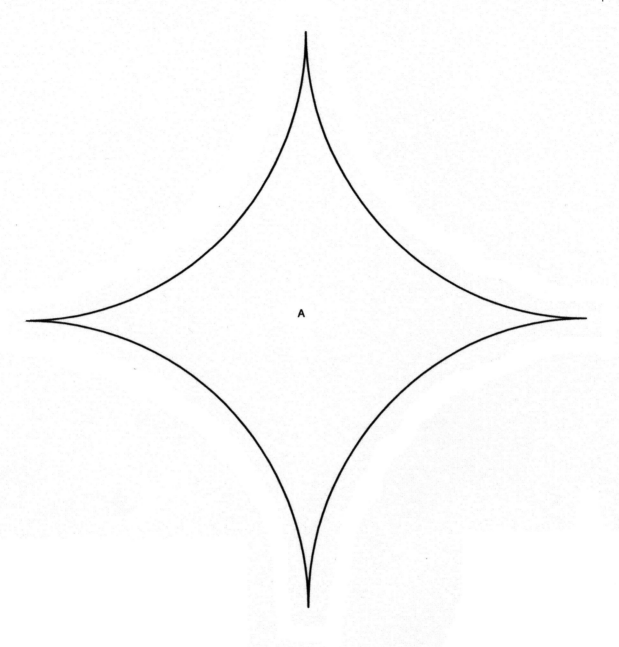

A

From The Kansas City Star, April 14, 1934: No. 349
Original size – 12"

A star for any quilter's crown is this one that is contributed by Mrs. Flossie Young of La Belle, Mo. She developed her quilt in black and white print, plain white, and orange. Remember to allow for seams.

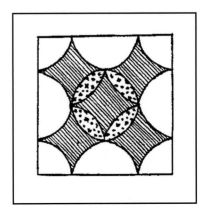

Quilt Takes Patriotic Hues

Appeared in The Star **January 23, 1957**

12" finished block

Fabric Needed
Red
White
Blue

Cutting Instructions

From the red, cut

1 – 7 1/4" square. Cut the square from corner to corner twice on the diagonal or cut 4 triangles using template B.

From the blue, cut

1 – 7 1/4" square. Cut the square from corner to corner twice on the diagonal or cut 4 triangles using template B.

2 – 3 7/8" squares. Cut each square from corner to corner once on the diagonal or cut 4 triangles using template A.

From the white, cut

1 – 7 1/4" square. Cut the square from corner to corner twice on the diagonal or cut 4 triangles using template B.

1 – 4 3/4" square or cut 1 square using template C.

To Make the Block (We'll sew this one together on the diagonal.)

Sew the red B triangles to the white B triangles as shown. Make 4.

Sew a red and white B unit to either side of the white center C square.

Now add a blue A triangle to each end as shown. This is the center strip of the block.

Sew a blue B triangle to either side of a red and white B unit as shown.

Add a blue A triangle. Make two units like this.

Sew the two strips you have made to the center to complete the block.

Quilt Takes Patriotic Hues Templates

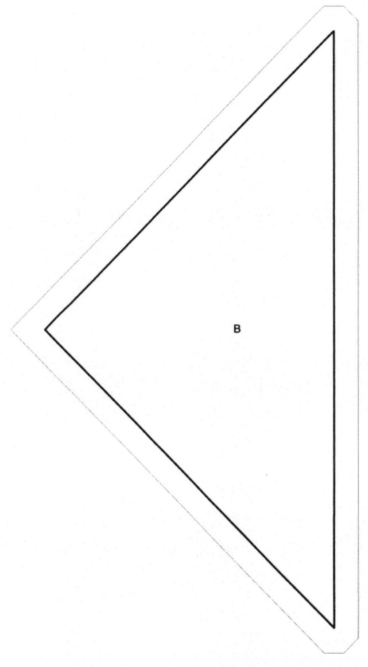

B

From The Kansas City Star, January 23, 1957: No. 1004
Original size – 9 1/2"

Developed in the colors of the United States flag, this quilt becomes an important part of a room's color planning. The designer is Emily Edna Bess, route 1, box 78, Poplar Bluff, Mo.

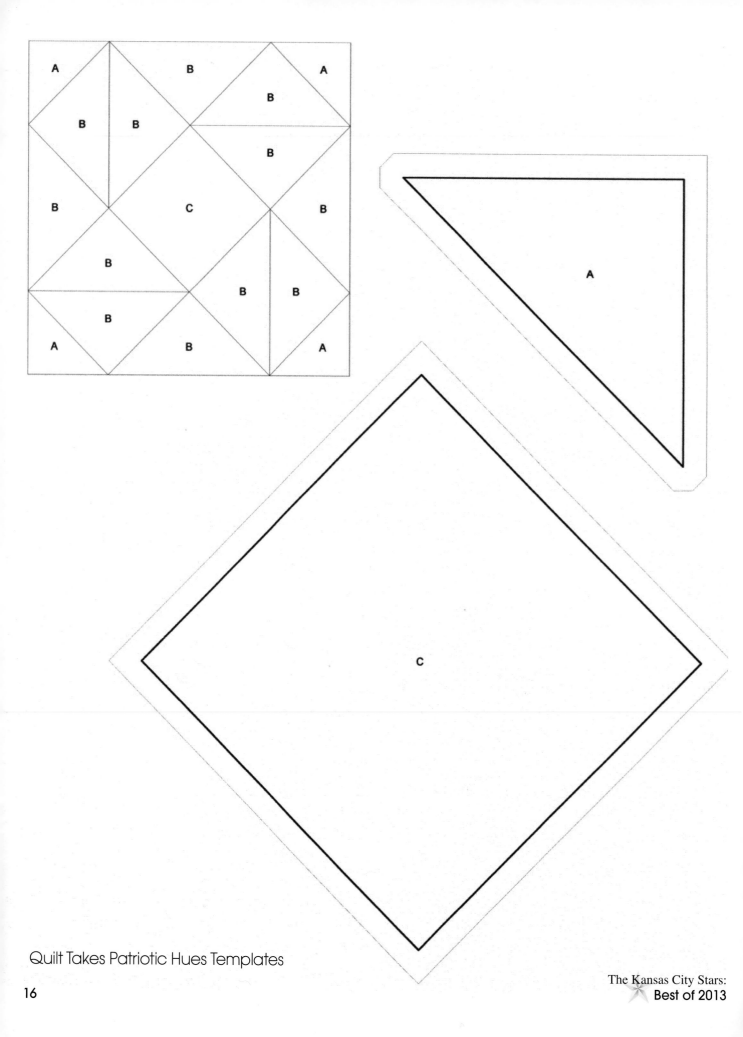

Quilt Takes Patriotic Hues Templates

Old English Wedding Ring

Appeared in The Star **December 28, 1955**

Cutting Instructions

From the green, cut

8 – 3 7/8" squares (or 16 triangles using template A).

From the medium pink print, cut

8 – 3 7/8" squares (or 16 triangles using template A).
8 – 3 1/2" squares (or use template B).

From the light pink fabric, cut

1 – 3 1/2" square (or use template B).

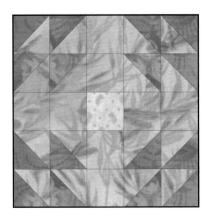

15" finished block

Fabric Needed
Medium pink print
Light pink print
Dark green

To Make the Block

You will need to make 16 green and medium pink half-square triangle units. To make the half-square triangles, draw a line from corner to corner on the reverse side of the medium pink 3 7/8" squares. Place a pink square atop a green square and sew 1/4" on either side of the drawn line. Using a rotary cutter, cut along the drawn line. Open each unit and press toward the darker fabric. If you cut your triangles separately, sew a green A triangle to a pink A triangle. Make 16 units.

Sew two half-square triangles to either side of a medium pink B square as shown below. Make 4 rows like this.

Sew two medium pink B squares to either side of the light pink B square. Make one row like this.

Sew the rows together as shown to complete the block.

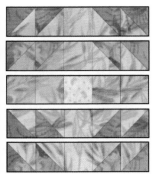

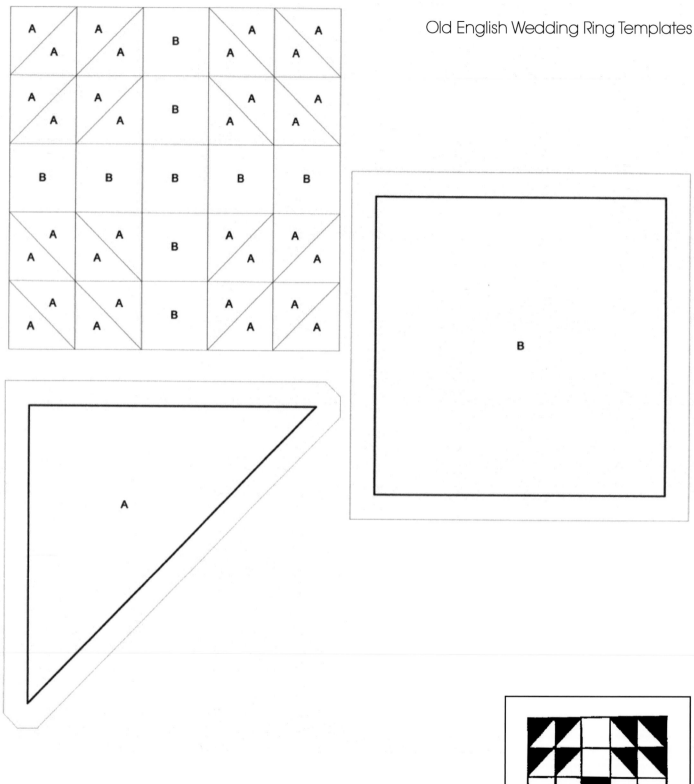

From The Kansas City Star, December 28, 1955: No. 971
Original size – 10"

Mrs. William Flottmann, 619 Klingsick lane, Washington, Mo., interprets the design
she has created thus: The center is the ring. The three pieces at the corners are the sets.

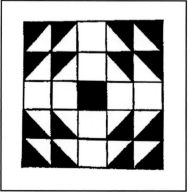

Indian Trail

Appeared in The Star **May 2, 1931**

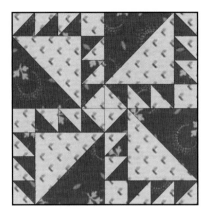

12" finished block

Fabric Needed
Red print
Cream shirting

Cutting Instructions

From the red print, cut

12 – 2 3/8" squares. Cut each square from corner to corner once on the diagonal or use template A.
2 – 5 3/8" squares. Cut each square from corner to corner once on the diagonal or use template C.

From the cream colored shirting, cut

12 – 2 3/8" squares. Cut each square from corner to corner once on the diagonal or use template A.
2 – 5 3/8" squares. Cut each square from corner to corner once on the diagonal or use template C.
4 – 2" squares or use template B.

To Make the Block

Sew a cream shirting 2 3/8" A triangle to a red print 2 3/8" A triangle to make a half-square triangle unit. Make 24.

Sew a cream shirting 5 3/8" C triangle to a red print 5 3/8" C triangle to make a half-square triangle unit. Make 4.

Sew three A half-square triangles together into a strip as shown. Make 4.

Sew three A half-square triangles together into a strip as shown. Make 4.

Sew a half-square triangle strip unit A to a C half-square triangle as shown.

Sew a cream shirting B square to the end of the half-square triangle strip.

Sew the strip to the top of the unit. Make four units like this.

Sew the four units together to complete the block.

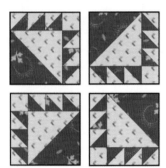

From The Kansas City Star, May 2, 1931: No. 168
Original size – 9"

This is a quilt with a myriad of names. "Indian Trail," "Forest Path," "Rambling Road," "North Wind" and "Irish Puzzle" are but a few of the names that have been given to this popular quilt. From the names we choose "Indian Trail" because of the unmistakable Swastika emblem in the block. Then, too, this pattern originated in the early days when the settlers were gradually moving westward and their contact with the Indians greatly influenced their daily lives. Piece four patches and set together as shown above, making a block nine inches square. Alternated with plain blocks the same size or set together with strips used for the figured triangles, white with a tiny figure, or dot for the other four, and green for the small triangles, a very pretty effect is obtained. Allow narrow seams.

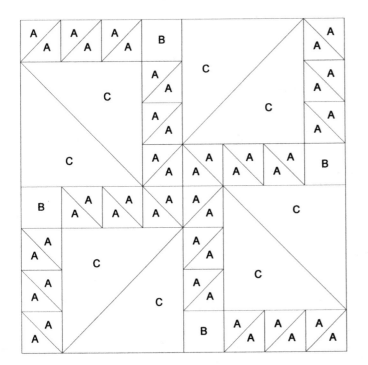

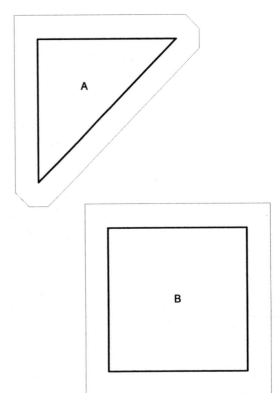

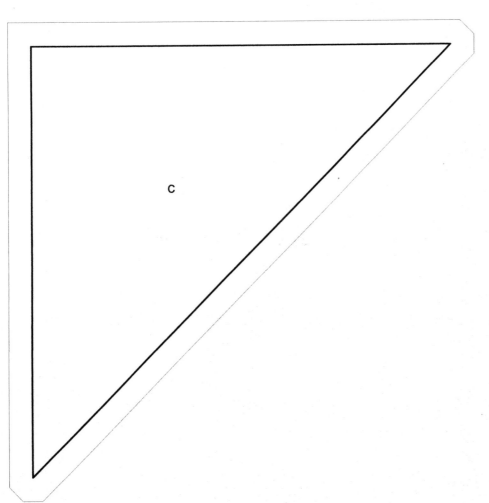

Buckeye Beauty

Appeared in The Star **November 15, 1939**

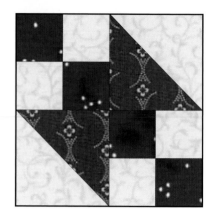

12" finished block

Fabric Needed
2 Navy blue prints
Cream

Cutting Instructions

From the one of the navy blue prints, cut
4 – 3 1/2″ squares (template A).

From the other navy blue print, cut
1 – 6 7/8″ square. Cut the square from corner to corner once on the diagonal or cut 2 triangles using template B.

From the cream fabric, cut
4 – 3 1/2″ squares (template A).
1 – 6 7/8″ square. Cut the square from corner to corner once on the diagonal or cut 2 triangles using template B.

To Make the Block

Sew a navy blue A square to a cream A square. Make 4. Sew the 2-patches together to make a 4-patch unit. Make 2 units.

Sew a navy blue B triangle to a cream B triangle. Make 2.

Sew a half-square triangle to a 4-patch unit. Make 2.

Sew the two rows together to complete the block.

"Blue Ridge Beauty" submitted by Judith Smith.

From The Kansas City Star, November 15, 1939: No. 599
Original size – 7"

Print and 1-tone blocks may be combined in this design, or two 1-tones may be used. Another choice is three different 1-tone blocks. The four squares running diagonally through the center may be of one color, the two center triangles of a harmonizing contrast, and the blocks, shown white in the pattern, may be left white or serve as the third number in the color scheme. Mrs. Jack I. Bonner, Jr., of Lehigh, Ok., who offers the design, developed her quilt in rose and blue.

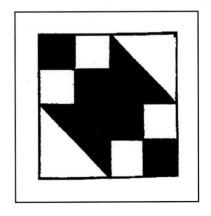

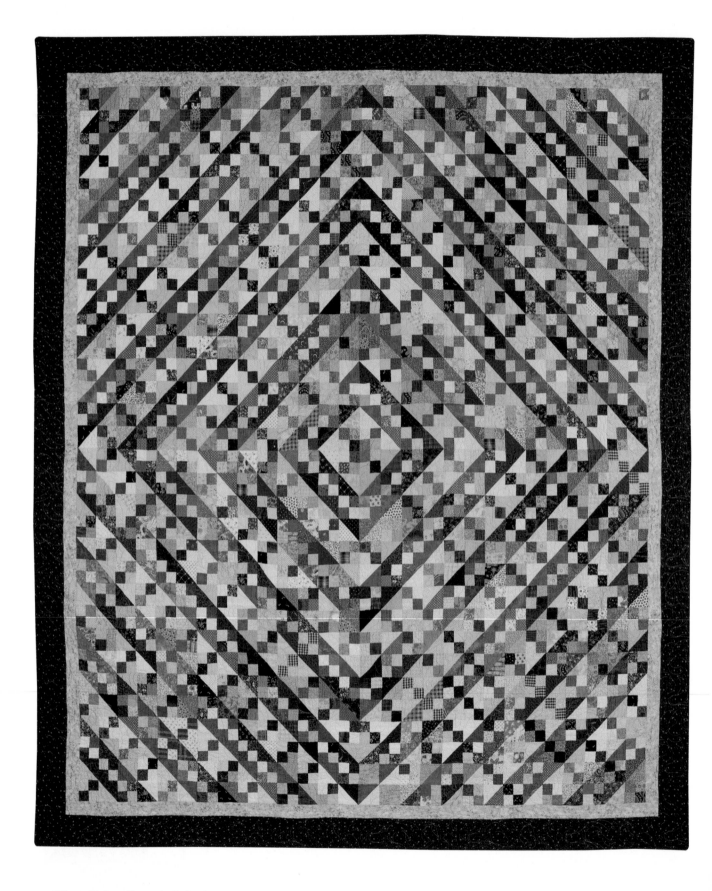

"Blue Ridge Beauty," designed by Bonnie Hunter, Winston Salem, N.C. Pieced by members of the Stitch By Stitch Quilt Guild, Marshall, Mo. Quilted by Janice Hollandsworth, Columbia, Mo.

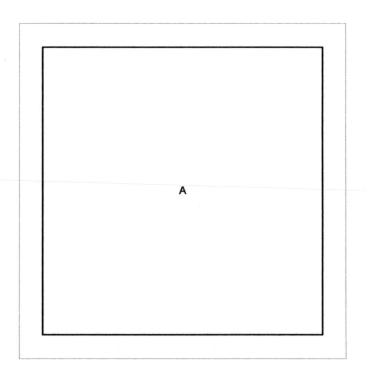

Buckeye Beauty Templates

Buckeye Beauty Templates

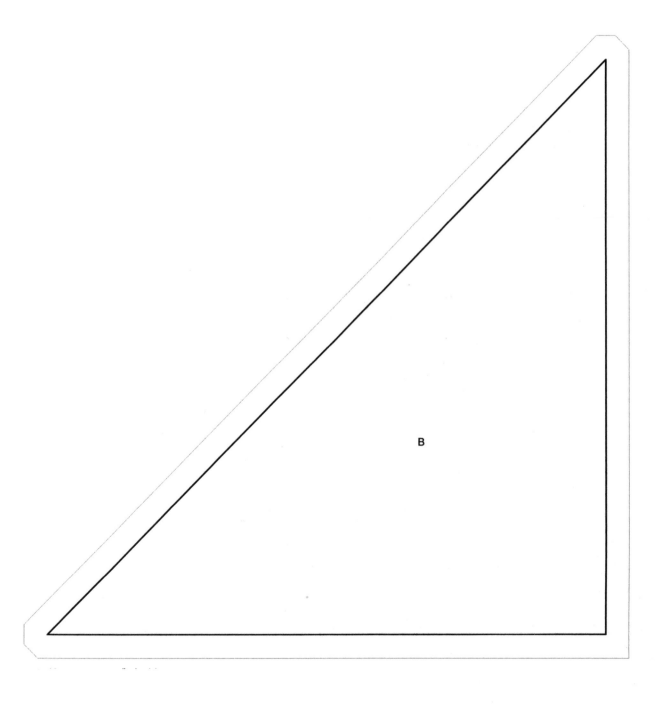

B

Car Wheel

Appeared in The Star **September 4, 1940**

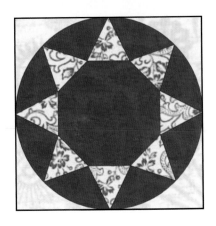

Cutting Instructions

From the grey fabric, cut
4 pieces using template A.

From the red fabric, cut
8 pieces using template D.
I octagon using template B.

From red/white print fabric, cut
8 pieces using template C.

12" finished block

Fabric Needed
Red
Red/white print
Grey

To Make the Block

Sew 4 of the red/white print C pieces to the hexagon as shown.

Sew a red D piece to either side of C red/white print. Make 4 of these units.

Sew a D/C/D unit to the center hexagon as shown. Each unit should be easily sewn in place between each of the C pieces.

The Kansas City Stars:
Best of 2013

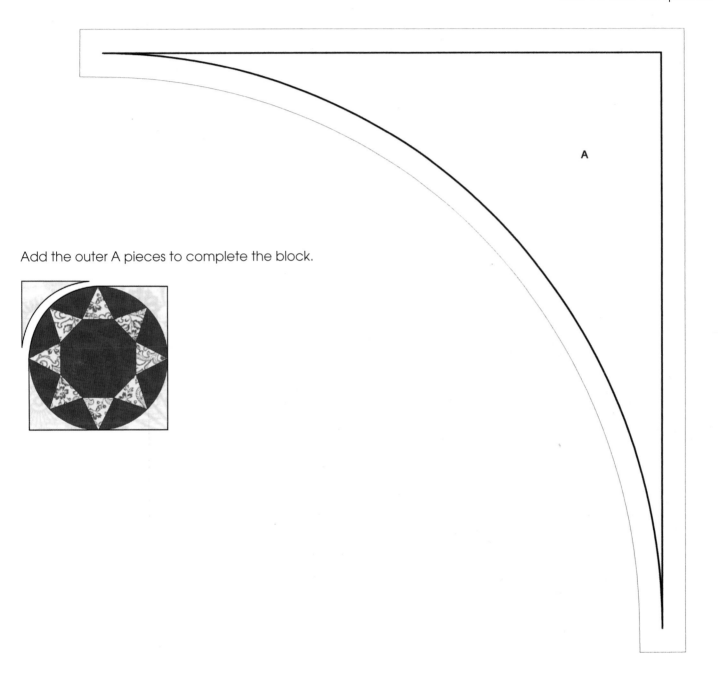

Add the outer A pieces to complete the block.

A

From The Kansas City Star, September 4, 1940: No. 626
Original size – 10 1/2"

The inspiration for a title for this design, created by Mrs. J. T. Dodd, route 2, Muskogee, Ok., may have come from observing gaily decorated parade cars. A print of small design would be preferable to a large one for this quilt top.

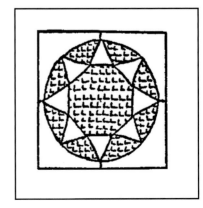

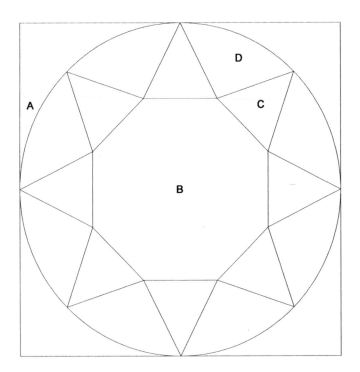

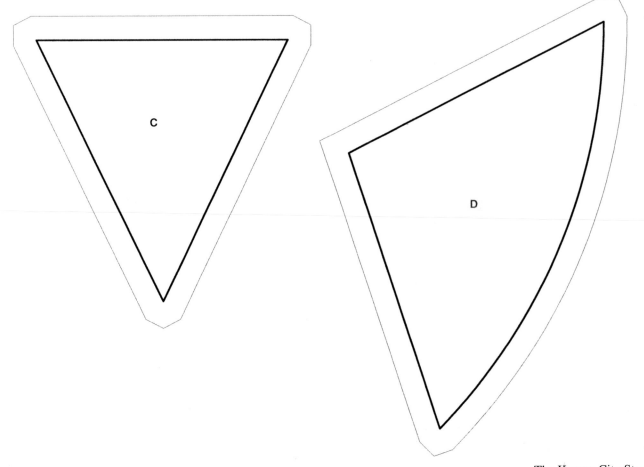

The Kansas City Stars:
Best of 2013

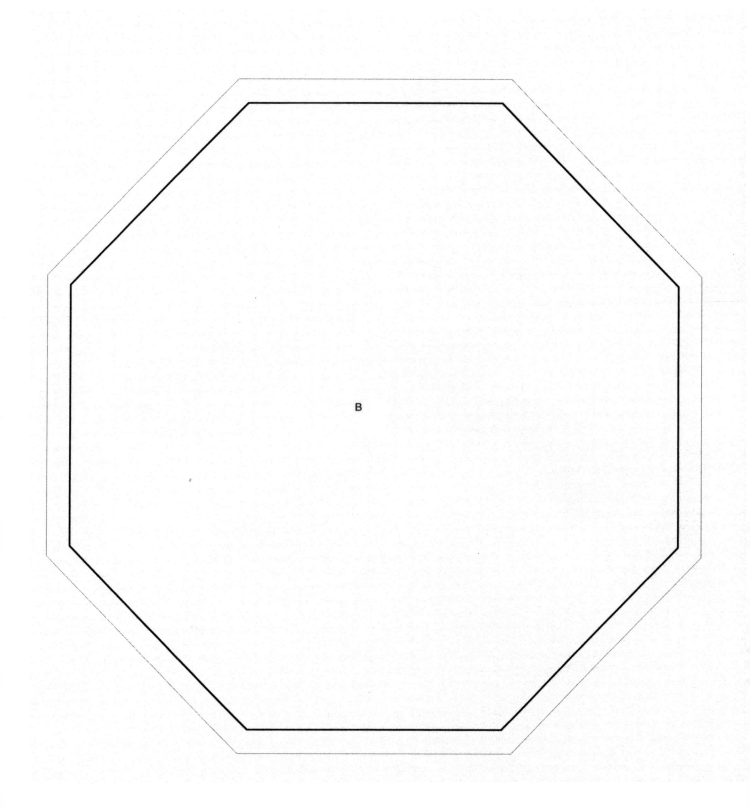

B

Bright Jewel

Appeared in The Star **September 28, 1949**

Cutting Instructions

From the cream fabric, cut

8 – 3 1/4" squares. Cut each square from corner to corner once on the diagonal or cut 16 triangles using template A.
1 – 2 7/8" square or cut 1 square using template B.

From the navy blue fabric, cut

8 – 3 1/4" squares. Cut each square from corner to corner once on the diagonal or cut 16 triangles using template A.
8 – 2 7/8" squares or cut 8 squares using template B.

Note: If you are rotary cutting, use a scant 1/4" seam allowance when you sew.

12" finished block

Fabric Needed
Navy blue
Cream

To Make the Block

Sew a cream A triangle to a navy blue A triangle to make a half-square triangle. Make 16.

Sew the half-square triangles and squares together into rows as shown below.

Sew the rows together to complete the block.

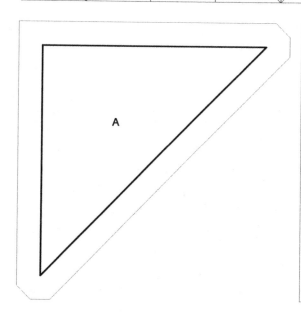

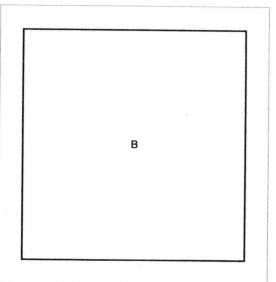

From The Kansas City Star, September 28, 1949: No. 858
Original size – 10"

The parts of this quilt block resemble the facets of a precious stone. Vivid one tones and small prints are interesting choices of color combinations. The block was designed by Mrs. Ida Grayson, route 2, Melvern, Kas.

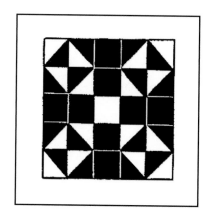

Double T

Appeared in The Star **November 28, 1928**

12" finished block

Fabric Needed
Tan
Blue/Tan print

Cutting Instructions

From the tan, cut

2 – 4 7/8″ squares. Cut the squares from corner to corner once on the diagonal or cut 4 triangles using template A.

2 – 5 1/4″ squares. Cut the squares from corner to corner twice on the diagonal or cut 8 triangles using template B.

From the blue/tan print fabric, cut

2 – 4 7/8″ squares. Cut the squares from corner to corner once on the diagonal or cut 4 triangles using template A.

8 – 2 7/8″ squares. Cut each square from corner to corner once on the diagonal or cut 16 triangles using template C.

1 – 4 1/2″ square or 1 square using template D.

To Make the Block

Sew a tan A triangle to a blue/tan print A triangle. Make 4 of these corner units and set aside for the moment.

Sew two blue/tan print C triangles to a tan B triangle as shown. This makes a flying geese unit. Make 8.

Sew two flying geese together. Make 4 of these sets.

Sew a corner unit to either side of a flying geese unit. Make two rows like this.

Sew a flying geese unit to either side of the D square. Make one row like this.

Sew the three rows together to complete the block.

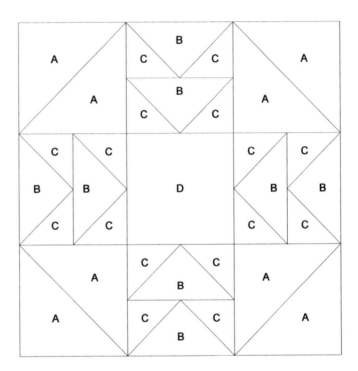

From The Kansas City Star, November 28, 1928: No. 11
Original size – 12"

The double T quilt pattern is another of those designs which is adapted for use on a patchwork pillow as well as for a counterpane. The completed block is twelve inches square. These 12-inch blocks may be set together for a quilt with alternate 12-inch plain squares between. Or it is very attractive with strips three inches wide of white or harmonizing color between the blocks, either continuing in unbroken lattice work or with 3-inch squares of a contrasting color at each corner. The patterns shown above are of the size needed for the quilt but do not allow for seams. To make cardboard patterns, trace these squares and triangles on cardboard and then cut out the patterns. Place cardboard patterns on the material and trace around these with a pencil line. When you cut them out, however, cut beyond the pencil line, allowing for a seam, and then sew back to the line when piecing. The smallest triangle pattern, from which sixteen print pieces are to be cut, should measure 3 inches on the long side, 2-1/8 inches on each of the two short sides.

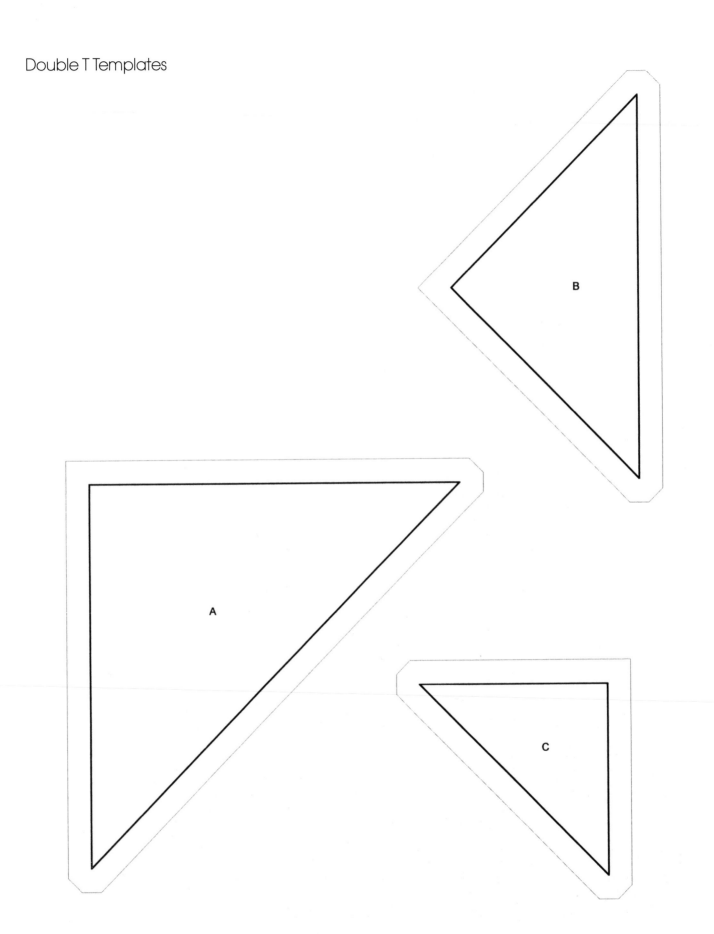

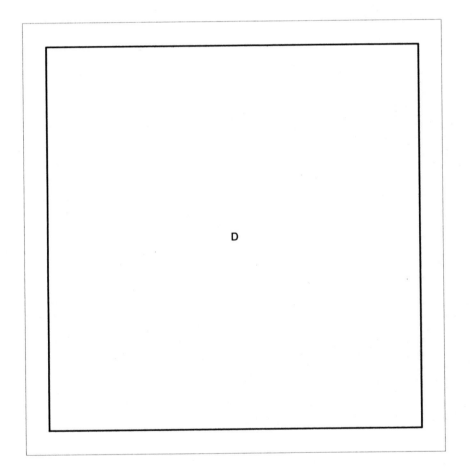

Cat's Cradle

Appeared in The Star **September 21, 1960**

9" finished block

Fabric Needed
Dark blue
Blue on white print

Cutting Instructions

From the dark blue fabric, cut

3 – 3 1/2" squares or use template B.
3 – 3 7/8" squares. Cut the squares from corner to corner once on the diagonal or cut 6 triangles using template A.

From the blue/white print fabric, cut

3 – 3 7/8" squares. Cut the squares from corner to corner once on the diagonal or cut 6 triangles using template A.

To Make the Block

Sew a dark blue A triangle to a blue/white print A triangle. Make 6 of these half-square triangle units.

Sew the half-square triangle units to the dark blue squares into three rows as shown below.

From The Kansas City Star, September 21, 1960: No. 1054
Original size – 9"

An attribute claimed for The Cat's Cradle is that when completed it is beautiful. To arrive at that state, the needlewoman must be certain that the diagonal lines are perfectly true. The contributor is Amelia Lampton, Aguilar, Colo.

Cat's Cradle Templates

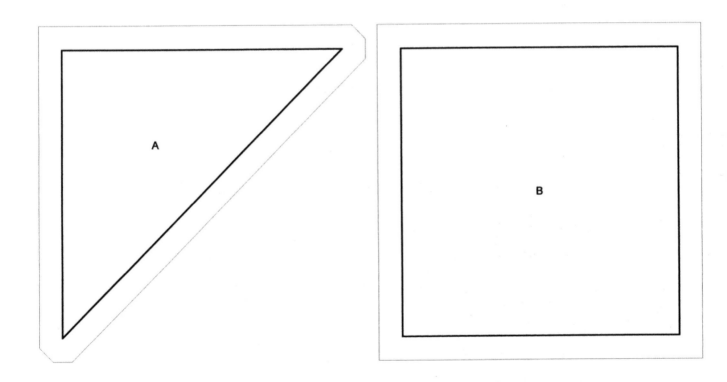

Goose in the Pond

Appeared in The Star **March 2, 1929**

15" finished block

Fabric Needed
Red
Cream

Cutting Instructions

From the red fabric, cut
6 – 3 7/8" squares. Cut each square from corner to corner once on the diagonal or cut 12 triangles using template A.
16 – 1 1/2" squares or use template C.
8 – 1 1/2" x 3 1/2" rectangles or use template D.

From the cream fabric, cut
6 – 3 7/8" squares. Cut each square from corner to corner once on the diagonal or cut 12 triangles using template A.
5 – 3 1/2" squares or use template B.
20 – 1 1/2" squares or use template C.
4 – 1 1/2" x 3 1/2" rectangles or use template D.

To Make the Block

Sew a cream A triangle to a red A triangle to make a half-square triangle unit. Make 12.

Sew the red C squares to the white C squares to make a 9-patch unit as shown. Make 4.

Sew a red D strip to either side of a cream D strip. Make 4.

Make the top row by sewing two half-square triangle units to either side of a cream B square.

The second row is made by sewing a half-square triangle unit to a 9-patch unit. Add a strip unit, then another 9-patch unit. End the row with a half-square triangle.

The center row is made by sewing a cream B square to a strip unit – add another cream B square, a strip unit and end with a cream square.

The fourth row is made by sewing a half-square triangle unit to a 9-patch unit. Add a strip unit, then aother 9-patch unit. End the row with a half-square triangle.

Make the last row by sewing two half-square triangle units to either side of a cream B square.

Sew the rows together to complete the block.

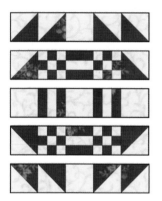

From The Kansas City Star, March 2, 1929: No. 24
Original size – 15"

Goose in the Pond is one of those old-fashioned names attached to many patchworks. It is composed of twenty-five 3-inch squares; five of them plain, twelve made of two triangles, four tiny ninepatches and four 3-layer strip squares. These make a block fifteen inches square. Set together with strips three inches wide and tiny ninepatches at the corners. It takes about sixteen blocks with borders to make a quilt; a wider border at the bottom of course. Cut the cloth a seam longer than the four patterns given here, as these are to be finished sizes. This is a good pattern for a patchwork pillow or tie-on chair seat covers.

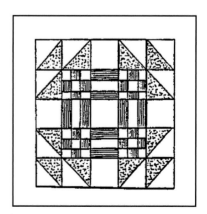

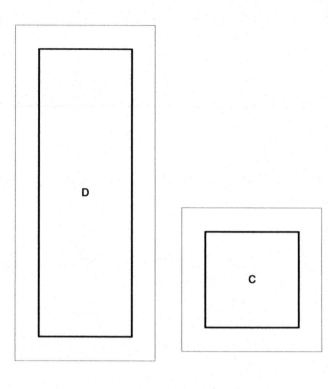

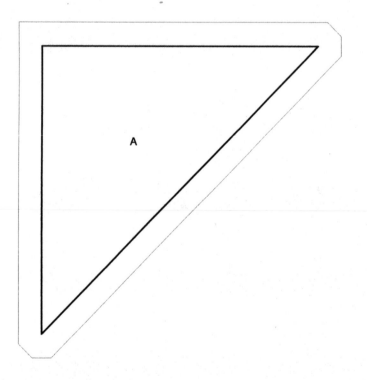

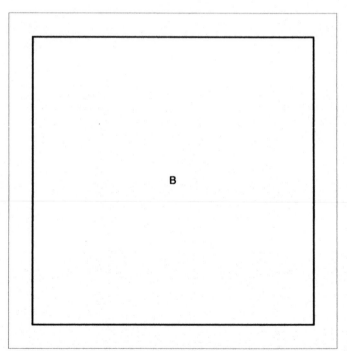

Goose in the Pond Templates

"Geese on the Pond," designed by Hearthside Quilts, Bedford, Va.
Pieced and quilted by Nancy E. Miller, Raymore, Mo.

The Kansas City Stars:
Best of 2013

"Goose in the Pond," designed by Hearthside Quilts, Bedford, Va.
Pieced by Sharon L. Tocchini, Danville, Calif. Quilted by Sandy Klop, Walnut Creek, Calif.

46

The Kansas City Stars:
Best of 2013

Bachelor's Puzzle

Appeared in The Star **August 8, 1931**

Cutting Instructions

From the light blue, cut

4 – 4 1/2" squares or use template C.

2 – 2 7/8" squares. Cut each square from corner to corner once on the diagonal or use template A.

1 – 3 5/16" square or use template E.

From the medium blue fabric, cut

4 diamonds using template B.

From the dark blue fabric, cut

4 diamonds using template D.

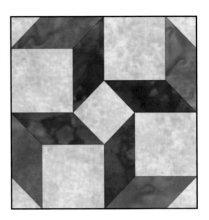

12" finished block

Fabric Needed
Light blue
Medium blue
Dark blue

To Make the Block

Sew a dark blue D diamond to a light blue C square.
Do not sew past your quarter-inch seam allowance.

Sew the medium blue B diamond to the C square, then miter the corner.

Add the A triangle as shown. Make four of these corner units.

Sew the corner units to the light blue E square. Some prefer to sew only the diamond portion in place, then going back and closing the seam allowances between each corner unit. Others will find it easier to complete each seam as they add a unit. Do what works best for you.

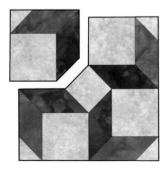

Bachelor's Puzzle Templates

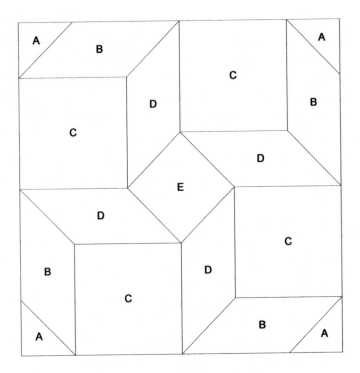

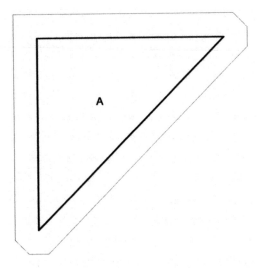

From The Kansas City Star, August 8, 1931: No. 182
Original size – 10 1/4"

Bachelors would not be the only ones puzzled over setting this block together, but what a cunning pattern it is with an individuality all of its own. To be effective it must be made of pieces with sharp color contrast, the four inside pieces preferable of a plain color, as shown above, and all of the blocks will be different. They are 10-1/4 inches square and are set together with plain blocks of same size. In piecing, start with center square and add the others in rotation. Allow for seams.

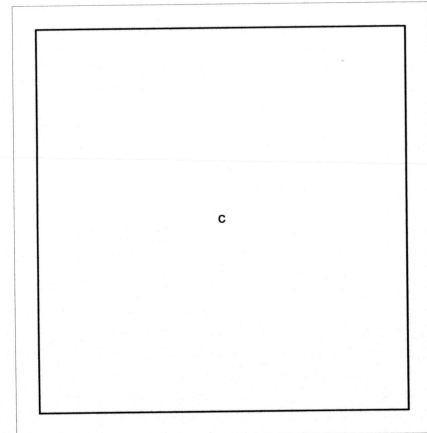

Bachelor's Puzzle Templates

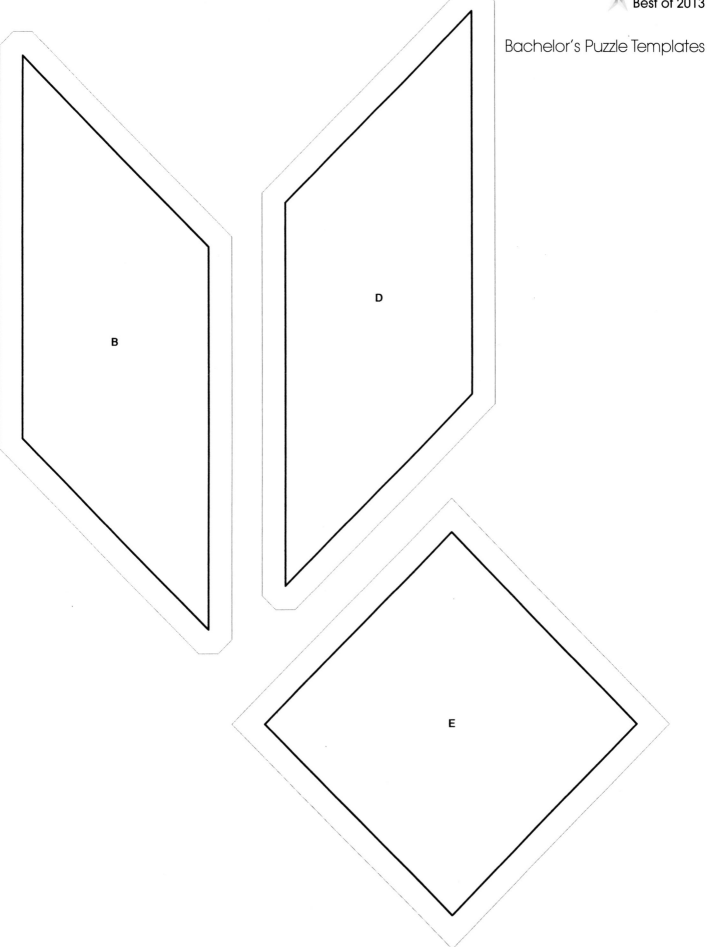

B

D

E

Old Maid's Puzzle

Appeared in The Star **December 22, 1928**

12" finished block

Fabric Needed
Cream
Light purple
Dark purple

Cutting Instructions

From the cream fabric, cut
4 – 3 1/2" squares or use template B.
5 – 3 7/8" squares. Cut each square from corner to corner once on the diagonal or use template A and cut 10 triangles.

From light purple, cut
2 – 3 7/8" squares. Cut each square from corner to corner once on the diagonal or use template A and cut 4 triangles.

From dark purple, cut
1 – 3 7/8" square. Cut the square from corner to corner once on the diagonal or use template A and cut 2 triangles.
1 – 6 7/8" square. Cut the square from corner to corner once on the diagonal or use template C and cut 2 triangles.

To Make the Block

Sew a cream A triangle to a light purple A triangle. Make 4 of these half-square triangle units.

Sew a light purple/cream half-square triangle unit to a cream B square. Make 4.

Sew the half-square triangles/square units together as shown to make one quadrant of the block. Make 2.

Sew a dark purple A triangle to a cream A triangle. Make 2 of these half-square triangles.

Sew a cream A triangle to two sides of the dark purple/cream half-square triangle. Make 2.

Add a dark purple C triangle as shown below. Make 2. Each is one quadrant of the block.

Sew the four quadrants together as shown to complete the block.

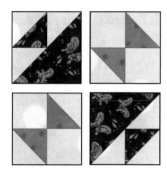

From The Kansas City Star, December 22, 1928: No. 14
Original size – 9"

One may be certain that "Old Maid's Puzzle" is a genuine antique quilt pattern because there hasn't been an "old maid" in a generation, and "bachelor girls" are not so easily puzzled. With this series of old-time quilt blocks, no additional pattern is needed. The triangles and square here given are the exact size of the finished parts in a block nine inches square. Cut cardboard patterns from these. Then place cardboard patterns on your material and trace around them with a pencil. When you cut the pieces out, allow for a seam and then sew back to the pencil line. (These patterns do not allow for seams.) This is quite a simple block to piece. There are four pieced squares, of two kinds. Just follow the pattern shown in the upper left of the sketch. The color scheme suggested uses odd scraps of pink, blue and green prints with white, but other color combinations are equally effective. When the 9-inch blocks are completed set them together, checkerboard style, alternating with plain blocks. Each color then will form a pattern in diagonals across the whole quilt.

Old Maid's Puzzle Templates

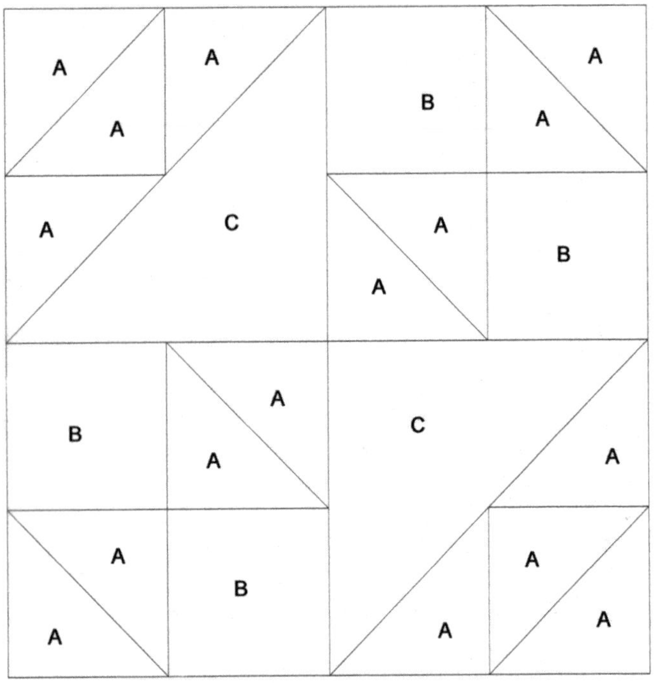

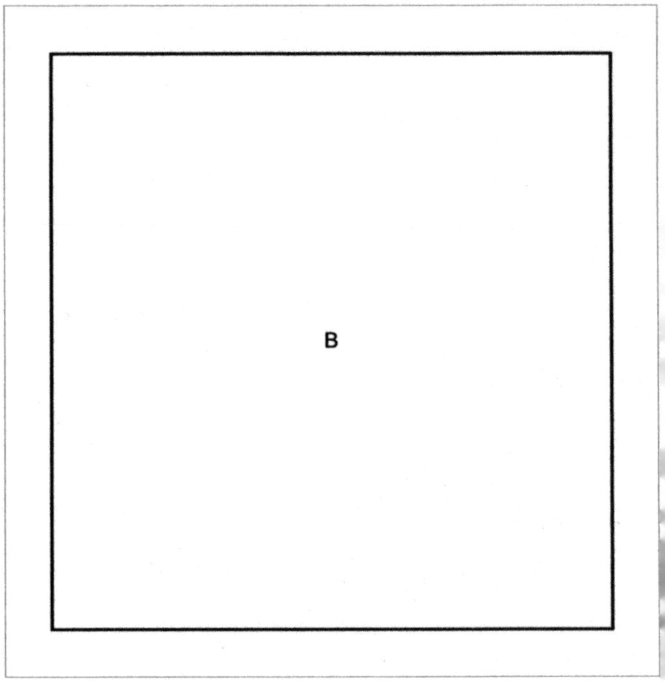

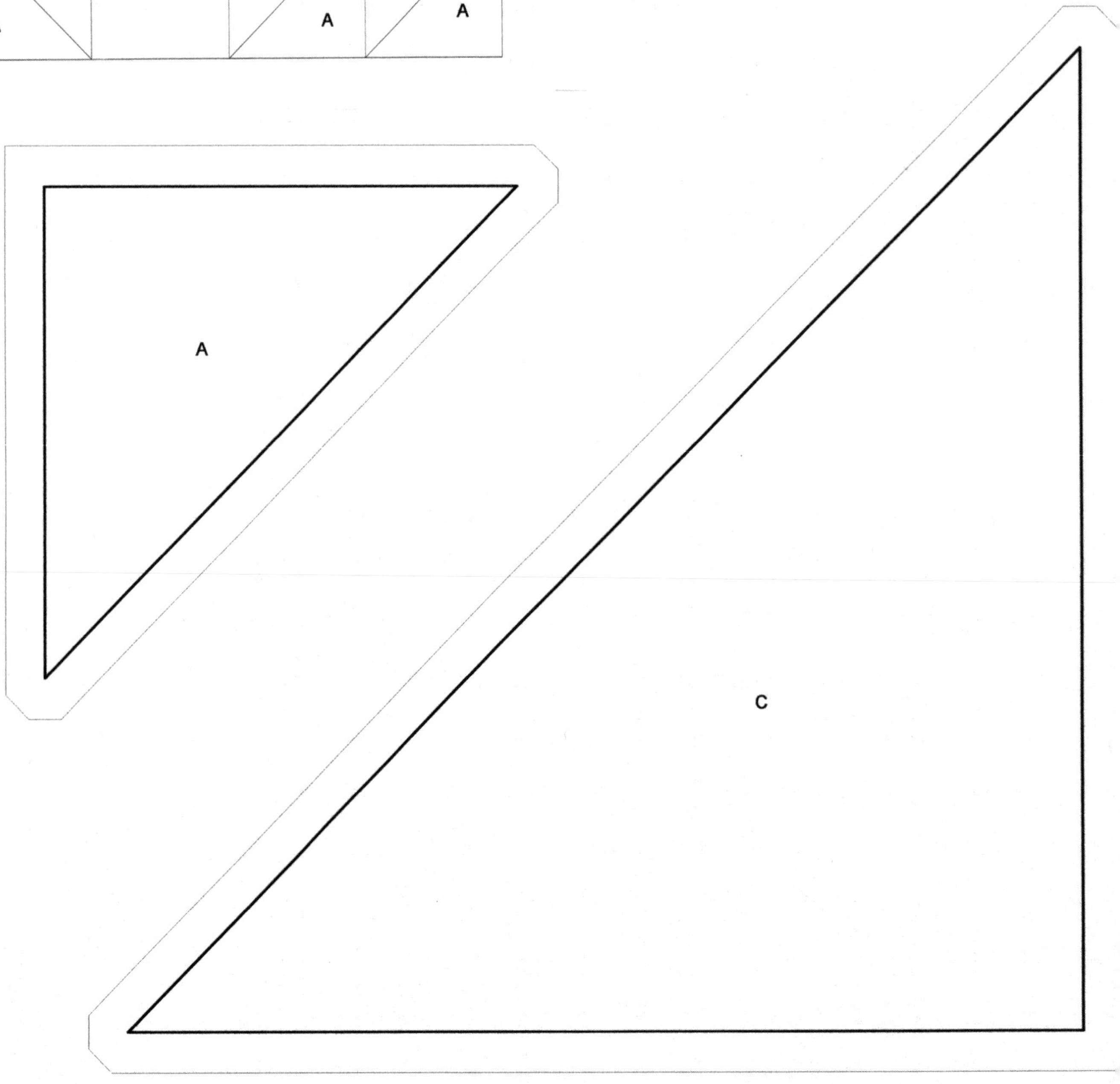

Jack in the Box

Appeared in The Star **July 6, 1929**

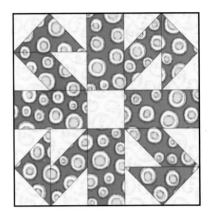

Cutting Instructions

From the cream colored fabric, cut

8 – 2 7/8" squares. Cut the squares from corner to corner once on the diagonal or cut 16 triangles using template A.

1 – 2 1/2" square or use template C.

From the red print fabric, cut

4 – 4 1/2" by 2 1/2" rectangles or use template B.

4 diamonds using template D.

1 – 5 1/4" square. Cut the square from corner to corner twice on the diagonal or cut 4 triangles using template E.

10" finished block

Fabric Needed
Cream
Red print

To Make the Block

Sew a cream A triangle to either side of a red E triangle.

Sew a cream A triangle to either side of a D diamond as shown below.

Sew the two units together to make a corner unit. Make 4.

Sew a corner unit to either side of a red B rectangle. Make 2 strips like this.

Sew a red rectangle to either side of a cream C square. Make one strip.

Sew the three strips together as shown to complete the block.

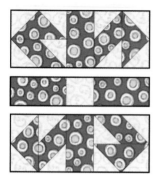

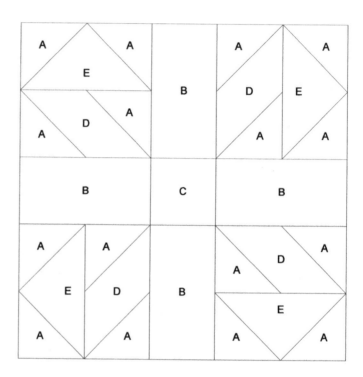

From The Kansas City Star, July 6, 1929: No. 42
Original size – 10"

Jack in the box is a crisp angular pattern almost as perky as its surprising name. The sketched block shows how easy it is to piece first the white triangles into a diamond, then two white triangles onto a red triangle, then wholemaking one corner square. Seams are not allowed so should be added to the sizes given. And right here may we put in a splendid suggestion for those who repeatedly wonder "How much material does it take to make a quilt?" by tracing onto brown paper as many patterns of each color as are called for in one block of the design and allowing seams between, quite accurate areas of cloth for one block may be estimated. Then it depends on the size you want the finished quilt and how the blocks are to be set together to determine the number of blocks to be used. Hence if it takes a 6-inch square of pink for one block and the quilt has eighteen blocks you would need half a yard of 36-inch material for that one color.

Jack in the Box Templates

Silent Star

Appeared in The Star **April 10, 1940**

12" finished block

Fabric Needed
Blue
Blue and cream shirting

Cutting Instructions

From the blue fabric, cut

2 – 4 7/8" squares. Cut each square from corner to corner once on the diagonal or cut 4 triangles using template A.

3 – 5 1/4" squares. Cut each square from corner to corner twice on the diagonal or cut 10 triangles using template B.

From the blue and cream shirting, cut

2 – 4 7/8" squares. Cut each square from corner to corner once on the diagonal or cut 4 triangles using template A.

3 – 5 1/4" squares. Cut each square from corner to corner twice on the diagonal or cut 10 triangles using template B.

To Make the Block

Sew a blue A triangle to a blue and cream shirting A triangle. Make 4.

Sew a blue B triangle to a B blue and cream shirting B triangle. Make 2 and sew the two together to make a quarter square triangle unit as shown below. Make 5.

Sew a half-square triangle unit to either side of a quarter-square triangle. Make two rows like this.

To make the center row, sew three quarter-square triangles together.

Sew the three rows together to complete the block.

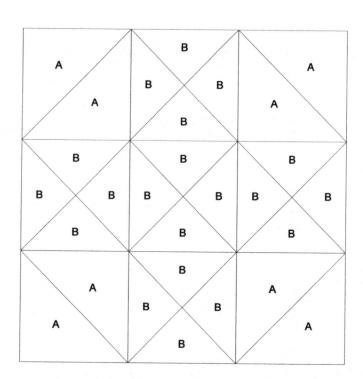

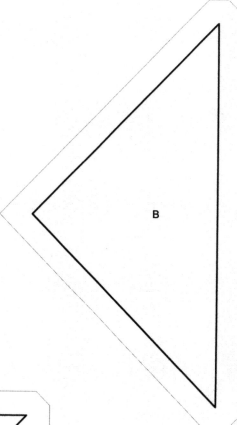

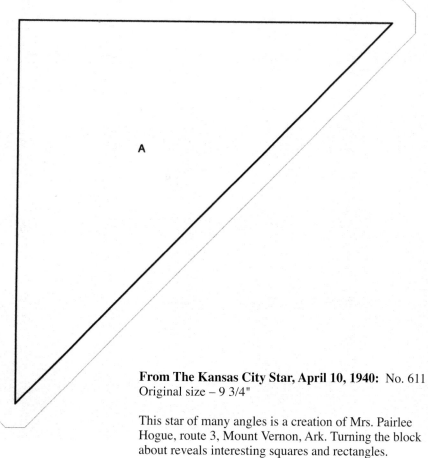

From The Kansas City Star, April 10, 1940: No. 611
Original size – 9 3/4"

This star of many angles is a creation of Mrs. Pairlee
Hogue, route 3, Mount Vernon, Ark. Turning the block
about reveals interesting squares and rectangles.

Martha Washington

Appeared in The Star **April 25, 1936**

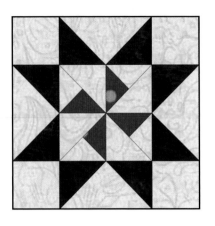

12" finished block

Fabric Needed
Cream
Navy blue
Red

Cutting Instructions

From the cream fabric, cut

4 – 3 1/2" squares or use template A.

1 – 7 1/4" square. Cut the square from corner to corner twice on the diagonal or cut 4 triangles using template B.

2 – 3 7/8" squares. Cut the squares from corner to corner once on the diagonal or cut 4 triangles using template C.

1 – 4 1/4" square. Cut the square from corner to corner twice on the diagonal or cut 4 triangles using template D.

From the navy blue fabric, cut

4 – 3 7/8" squares. Cut the squares from corner to corner once on the diagonal or cut 8 triangles using template C.

From the red fabric, cut

1 – 4 1/4" square. Cut the square from corner to corner twice on the diagonal or cut 4 triangles using template D.

To Make the Block

Sew a red D triangle to a cream D triangle. Make 4.

Add a cream C triangle. Make 4 of these for the center of the block.

Sew the center units together as shown.

Sew a navy blue C triangle to two sides of a cream B triangle as shown. Make 4 of these flying geese units.

Sew a flying geese unit to either side of the center.

The Kansas City Stars:
Best of 2013

Sew a cream A square to either end of a flying geese unit as shown. Make two strips like this.

Sew a strip to the top and one to the bottom of the center to complete the block.

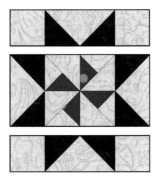

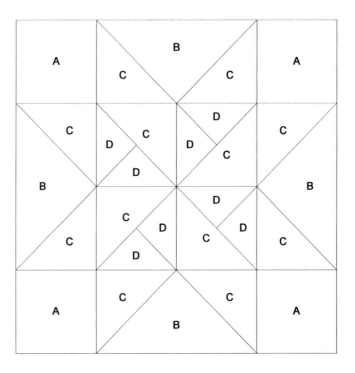

Appeared in The Star April 25, 1936: No. 452
Original size - 11"

This design for a "Martha Washington" quilt block was contributed by Mrs. Ina Lincoln, Corning, Ark., who says it is best developed in a 2-color combination.

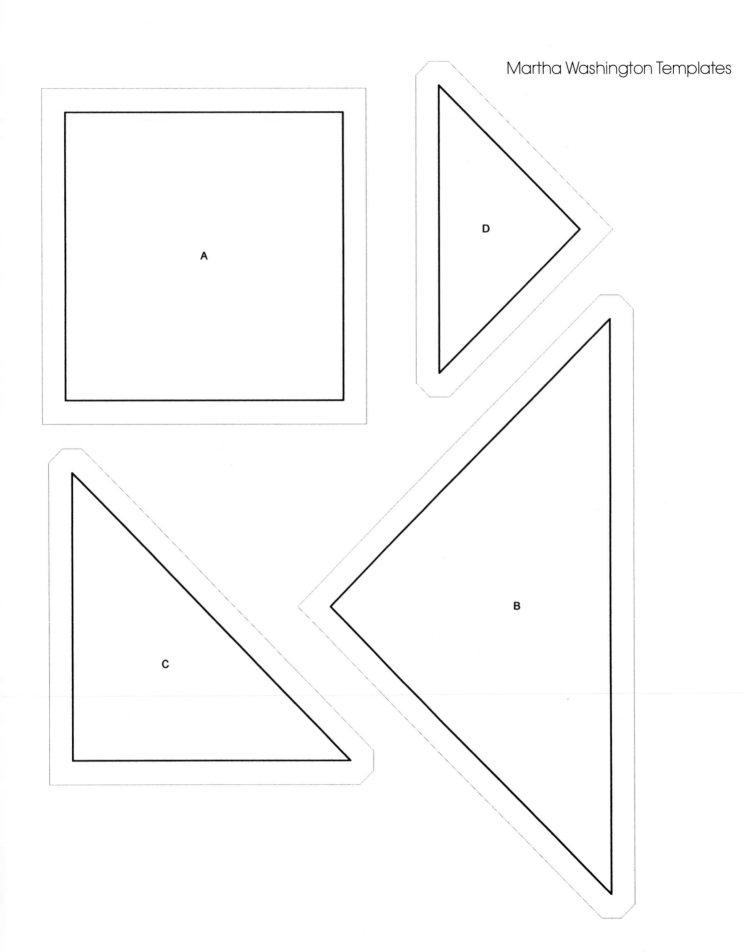

"Plaid Pinwheels and Stars," by Barbara Dahl, Bellingham, Wa.

"Plaid Pinwheels and Stars," pieced by Barbara Dahl, Bellingham, Wa.
Quilted by Debbie Mickschl, Birch Bay, Wa.

Gretchen

Appeared in The Star **July 16, 1932**

Cutting Instructions

From the red fabric, cut

4 – 2 7/8" squares. Cut each square from corner to corner once on the diagonal or cut 8 triangles using template A.
2 – 4 7/8" squares. Cut each square from corner to corner once on the diagonal or cut 4 triangles using template B.
4 pieces using template C.

From the cream fabric, cut

4 – 2 7/8" squares. Cut each square from corner to corner once on the diagonal or cut 8 triangles using template A.
2 – 4 7/8" squares. Cut each square from corner to corner once on the diagonal or cut 4 triangles using template B.
4 pieces using template C.

To Make the Block

Sew a red A triangle to each end of a cream C piece. Make 4.

Sew the A/C/A piece to a red B triangle. Make 4.

Sew a cream A triangle to each end of a red C piece. Make 4.

Sew the A/C/A piece to a cream B triangle. Make 4.

Sew 2 units together as shown to make up 1 quadrant of the block. Make 4.

Sew the 4 quadrants together to complete the block.

12" finished block

Fabric Needed
Red
Cream

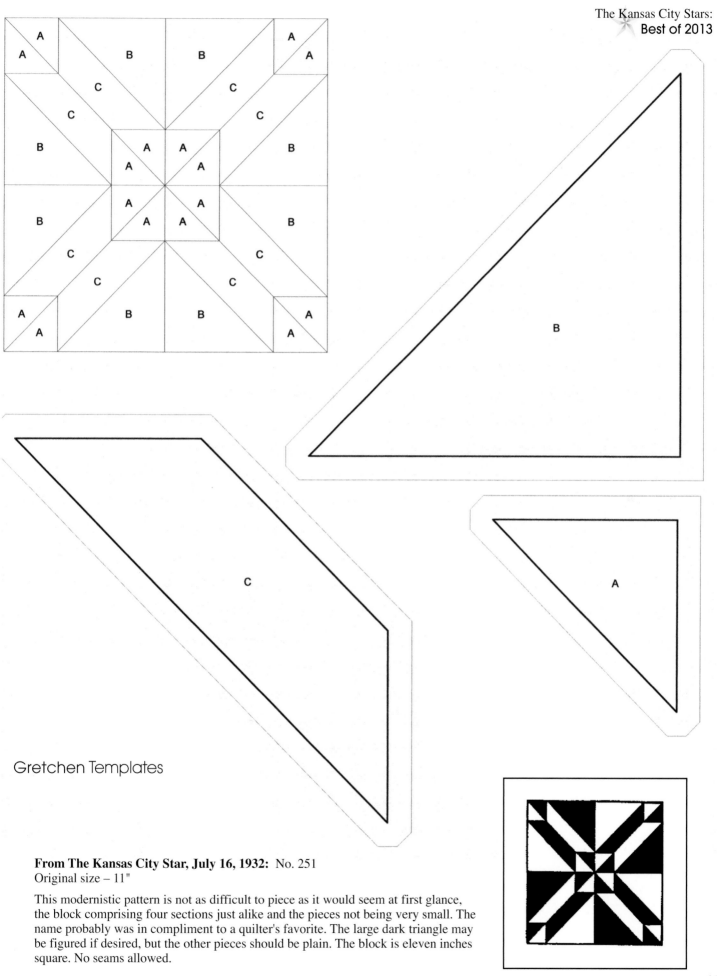

Gretchen Templates

From The Kansas City Star, July 16, 1932: No. 251
Original size – 11"

This modernistic pattern is not as difficult to piece as it would seem at first glance, the block comprising four sections just alike and the pieces not being very small. The name probably was in compliment to a quilter's favorite. The large dark triangle may be figured if desired, but the other pieces should be plain. The block is eleven inches square. No seams allowed.

Arkansas Star

Appeared in The Star **January 14, 1933,**
March 4, 1933 and October 6, 1948

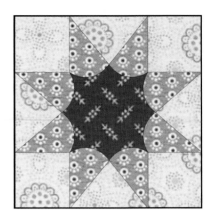

12" finished block

Fabric Needed
Dark blue
Medium blue
Cream/blue print

Cutting Instructions

From the dark blue fabric, cut
1 piece using template E.

From the medium blue fabric, cut
4 pieces using template C.
4 pieces using template D.

From the cream/blue print, cut
4 squares using template A.
4 triangles using template B.

Note: This block would be easiest to piece if done by hand rather than using the machine. It's beautiful and well worth the effort.

To Make the Block

Stitch the medium blue C and D pieces to the center E piece along the curved edges.

You will have to inset the cream/blue print A and B pieces in place as shown to complete the block.

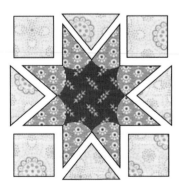

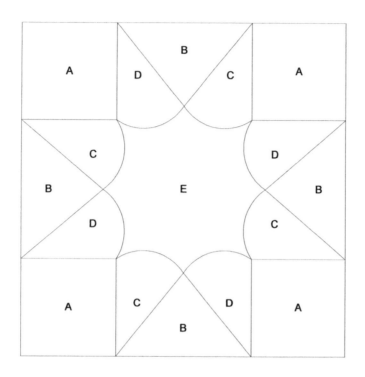

From The Kansas City Star, January 14, 1933, March 4, 1933, and October 6, 1948:
Number 288, 295, and 837
Original size – 10"

Number 288 – This pattern should be cut carefully allowing for seams. Use care with the curved line. This is a variation of "Rising Sun."

Number 295 – The simplicity and beauty of this quilt will encourage the quilter who enjoys the designs of historic origin. This one came from Virginia originally and was changed to the curved lines by an Arkansas woman who desired to show that she was an expert and could improve on the old star design which had no curved lines.

Number 837 – Eight points has this Arkansas Star. To accent the points, choose a 1-tone contrasting material for the background and fabric of small design for the center piece.

Arkansas Star Templates

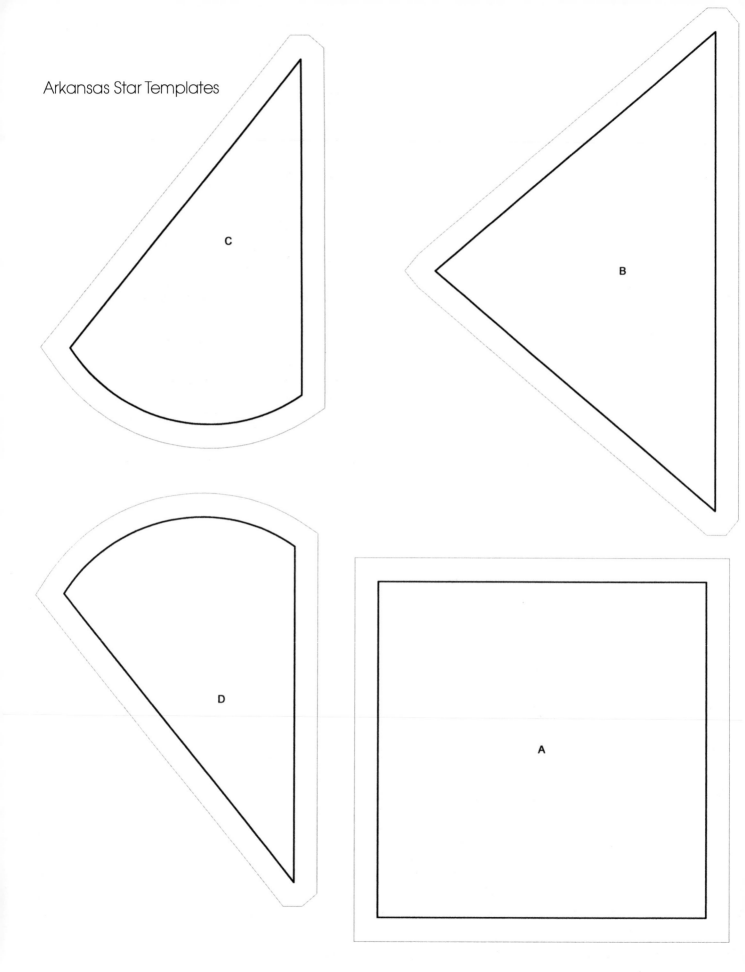

C

B

D

A

E

Hanging Basket

Appeared in The Star **August 11, 1937**

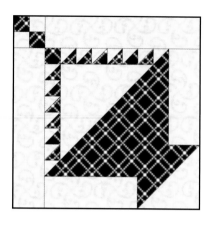

12" finished block

Fabric Needed
Black
Cream

Cutting Instructions

From the black fabric, cut

3 – 1 1/2" squares or use template A.

6 – 1 7/8" squares. Cut each square from corner to corner once on the diagonal or cut 12 triangles using template E.

1 – 2 7/8" square. Cut the square from corner to corner once on the diagonal or cut 2 triangles using template F.

1 – 8 7/8" square. Cut the square from corner to corner once on the diagonal. Because of page constraints, there is no template given for this piece. For the purpose of clarity, we will call it triangle H. You will have one triangle left over which you can set aside for another project.

From the cream fabric, cut

2 – 1 1/2" squares or use template A.

2 – 2 1/2" x 10 1/2" rectangles or use template B.

2 – 2 1/2" x 6 1/2" rectangles or use template C.

1 – 4 7/8" square. Cut the square from corner to corner once on the diagonal or cut one triangle using template D - If you cut the square, you will have one triangle left over for another project.

7 – 1 7/8" squares. Cut each square from corner to corner once on the diagonal or cut 14 triangles using template E.

1 – 6 7/8" square. Cut the square from corner to corner once on the diagonal or cut 1 triangle using template G - You will have one triangle left over for another project.

To Make the Block

Use 2 cream 1 1/2" A squares and 2 black 1 1/2" A squares to stitch together a 4-patch unit as shown below. Set aside.

Sew a black B triangle to a cream B triangle to make a half-square triangle unit. Make 12.

Sew 6 black and cream half-square triangles together oriented as shown. End the row with a cream B triangle.

Sew the remaining half-square triangles together oriented as shown. Add a cream B triangle to one end and the remaining black A square to the other. See the diagram below.

Sew the half-square triangle strips to the cream G triangle. This makes the top portion of the basket.

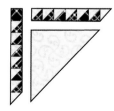

To make the bottom portion of the basket block, sew a cream C rectangle to a black F triangle. You will need to make two of these components but they must be mirror images as shown.

Sew the C/F units to the black H triangle as shown.

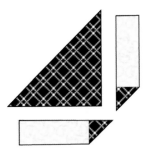

Add the cream D triangle to complete the basket base.

Sew the basket base to the basket top.

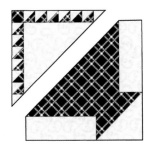

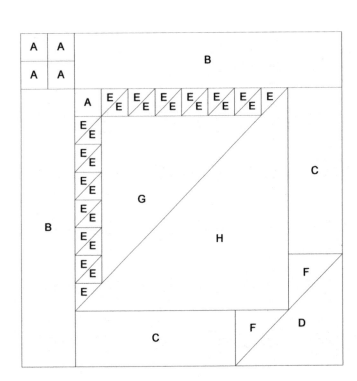

Add a cream B rectangle to the side of the basket as shown.

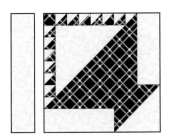

Sew the black and cream 4-patch unit to the remaining cream B rectangle.

Add the strip to the top of the basket to complete the block.

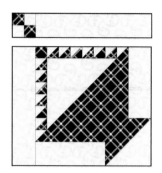

Hanging Basket Templates

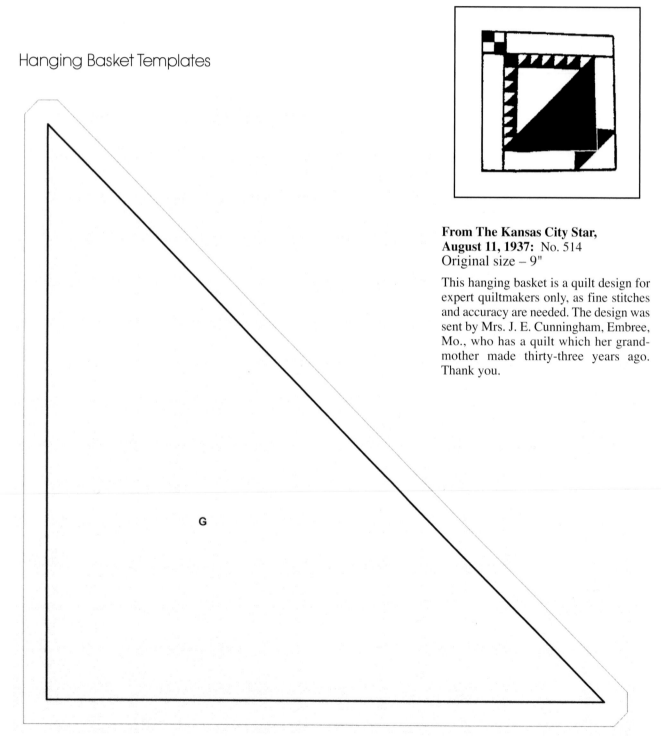

G

From The Kansas City Star,
August 11, 1937: No. 514
Original size – 9"

This hanging basket is a quilt design for expert quiltmakers only, as fine stitches and accuracy are needed. The design was sent by Mrs. J. E. Cunningham, Embree, Mo., who has a quilt which her grandmother made thirty-three years ago. Thank you.

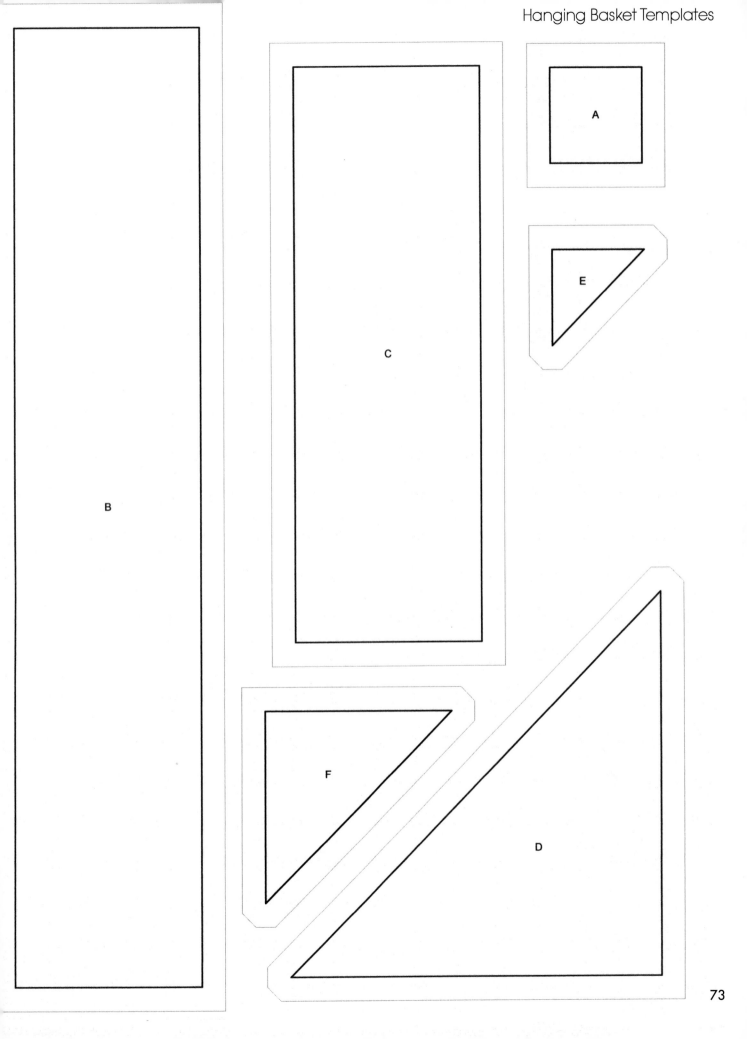

Clay's Choice

Appeared in The Star **July 26, 1930 and October 9, 1937**

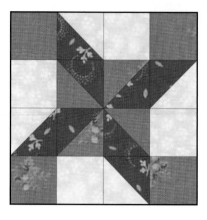

Cutting Instructions

From the light tan, cut
4 – 3 1/2" squares or use template A.
2 – 3 7/8" squares. Cut the squares from corner to corner once on the diagonal or cut 4 triangles using template B.

From the dark tan fabric, cut
4 – 3 1/2" squares or use template A.
2 – 3 7/8" squares. Cut the squares from corner to corner once on the diagonal or cut 4 triangles using template B.

From the dark brown fabric, cut
4 – 3 7/8" squares.

12" finished block

Fabric Needed
Light tan
Dark brown
Dark tan

To Make the Block

Sew a light tan B triangle to a dark brown B triangle. Make 4 half-square triangle units in this color way.

Sew a dark tan B triangle to a dark brown B triangle. Make 4 half-square triangle units in this color way.

Sew a dark tan A square to a dark brown/tan half-square triangle. Add a light tan A square and a dark tan A square to complete the row. Make two.

Sew a light tan A square to a dark tan/dark brown half-square triangle unit. Add another dark tan/dark brown half-square triangle as shown. Complete the row by adding a dark brown/light tan half-square triangle. Make two.

Sew the four rows together to complete the block.

Clay's Choice Templates

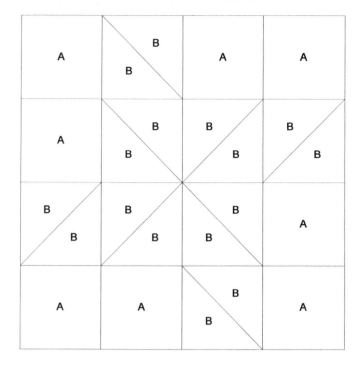

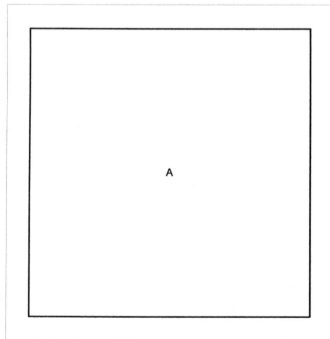

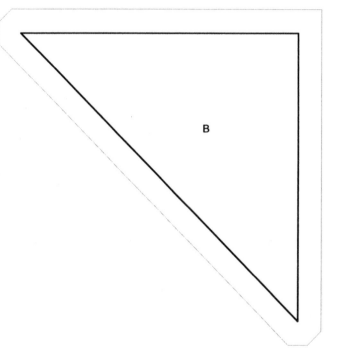

From The Kansas City Star, July 26, 1930: No. 107
Original size – 10"

Quilt patterns are ever so much more interesting if one knows their stories. "Clay's Choice" is a very lovely block in its own right, but when it is traced back to the bitter Calhoun or Clay days one finds it as Harry's Star or Clay's choice in the soft brown tone prints of prewar days. Then it becomes "Henry of the West" as the tide of empire surges westward and another generation forgets Clay entirely and calls it "Star of the West." "Clay's Choice" or "Star of the West" is easily pieced if developed as shown in the sketch. It might be set together with alternate plain squares of either white or yellow.

Also published October 9, 1937: No. 524

The revival of old patterns gives a new generation of quilters an opportunity to use the patterns again. This is "Clay's Choice."

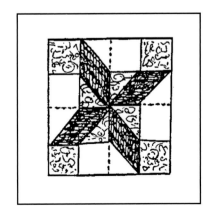

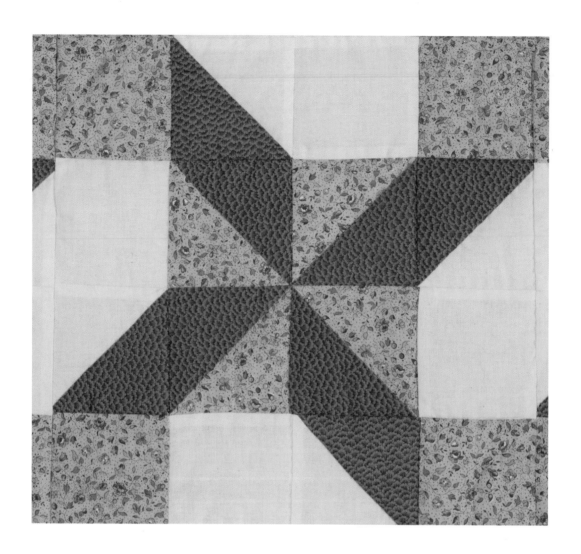

"Clay's Choice" by Rae B. Clay, Lower Bank, N.J.

"Clay's Choice," designed and pieced by Rae B. Clay, Lower Bank, N.J.
Quilted by Shirley Nash, Colebrook, N.H.

Jacob's Ladder

Appeared in The Star **November 7, 1928 and October 13, 1934**

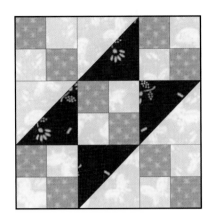

Cutting Instructions

From the black fabric, cut

2 – 4 7/8" squares. Cut each square from corner to corner once on the diagonal or cut 4 triangles using template B.

From the gold fabric, cut

10 – 2 1/2" squares or use template A.

From the cream fabric, cut

2 – 4 7/8" squares. Cut each square from corner to corner once on the diagonal or cut 4 triangles using template B.
10 – 2 1/2" squares or use template A.

12" finished block

Fabric Needed
Black
Gold
Cream

To Make the Block

Sew a cream B triangle to a black B triangle to make a half-square triangle unit. Make 4.

Sew 2 gold and 2 cream 2 1/2" A squares together to make a 4-patch unit. Make 5.

Sew a 4-patch unit to either side of a black and cream half-square triangle unit.

Sew a half-square triangle unit to either side of a 4-patch unit to make the center row.

Sew a 4-patch unit to either side of a black and cream half-square triangle unit.

Sew the three rows together as shown to complete the block.

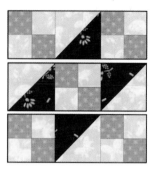

From The Kansas City Star, November 7, 1928: No. 8
Original size – 13 1/2"

The names in this old-fashioned quilt series are almost as interesting as the patterns themselves. Today it is the Jacob's Ladder pattern which is given. The blocks are rather large when pieced together, thirteen and a half inches square. Each of these large blocks is composed of nine little pieced blocks. And these little blocks are in turn divided into two groups - five four-patches, and four triangle squares - see the diagram above. The patterns for the triangle and square are given above. These do not allow for seams. Make the patterns by cutting the square and triangle out of cardboard. Then place the cardboard pattern on your material and draw around it with a pencil. Now when you cut out the pieces, be sure to allow enough extra for a seam, but when you sew it - sew back on the pencil line. Piece the squares and triangles together as shown, alternating dark with light. When the large 13-1/2-inch squares are completed put these together alternately with squares of unbleached material, or whatever light colored fabric is used. Jacob's Ladder is a simple pattern to cut, but, like the others, has to be set together accurately to make perfect patchwork. A file of these quilt patterns which are published in The Star each week might be kept by putting each set of cardboard patterns in an envelope upon which is pasted the sketch and description.

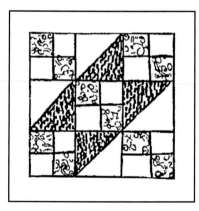

From The Kansas City Star, October 13, 1934. No. 375
Original size - 13 1/2"

This pattern is the gift from Miss Evelyn Baster, a quilt fan. It is a new expression of a very old theme, Jacob's Ladder, attractive in any two colors. Allow for seams.

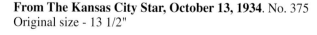

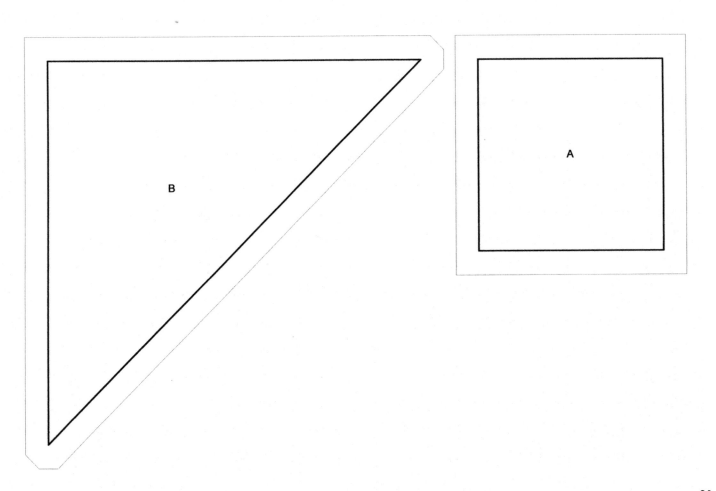

Flower Pot

Appeared in The Star **January 16, 1937**

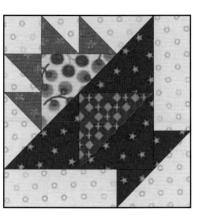

Cutting Instructions

From the tan fabric, cut

2 - 2 7/8" x 7 11/16" rectangles (template D.)

1 – 5 5/8" square. Cut the square from corner to corner once on the diagonal. You will have one triangle left over for another project or cut 1 triangle using template E.

1 – 2 7/8" square or use template A.

1 – 3 1/4" square. Cut the square from corner to corner once on the diagonal or cut two triangles using template B.

1 – 6" square. Cut the square from corner to corner twice on the diagonal (you will have two triangles left over for another project) or cut two triangles using template C.

From the double pink fabric, cut

2 – 3 1/4" squares. Cut the squares from corner to corner once on the diagonal or cut 4 triangles using template B.

From the medium pink prink, cut

1 – 5 5/8" square. Cut the square from corner to corner once on the diagonal. You will have one triangle left over for another project or cut 1 triangle using template E.

From the medium blue print, cut

1 – 5 5/8" square. Cut the square from corner to corner once on the diagonal. You will have one triangle left over for another project or cut 1 triangle using template E.

From the dark blue fabric, cut

2 – 5 5/8" squares. Cut the squares from corner to corner once on the diagonal. You will have one triangle left over for another project or cut 3 triangles using template E.

1 – 3 1/4" square. Cut the square from corner to corner once on the diagonal or cut 2 triangles using template B.

12" finished block

Fabric Needed
Tan
Dark blue
Medium blue
Double pink
Medium pink print

To Make the Block

Sew the dark blue B triangles to the tan D rectangles as shown.

Sew a double pink B triangle to one side of a tan C triangle. Make two as shown below.

Sew a tan B triangle to a double pink B triangle. Make two.

Sew the medium blue E triangle to a dark blue E triangle.

Add a dark blue E triangle to either side of the half-square triangle unit you have just completed.

Stitch the D/B units to the base of the basket as shown.

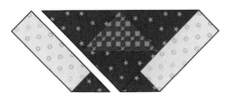

Add a tan E triangle to finish the base and set aside for the moment.

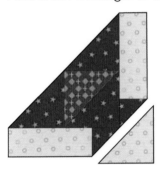

Sew a tan/pink C/B unit to a tan and pink half-square triangle unit as shown. Make two.

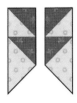

Sew one to the side of the pink print E triangle.

Sew the tan A square to the remaining strip as shown.

Add this strip to the E triangle unit as show. This completes the top of the basket.

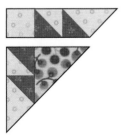

Sew the two basket parts together to complete the block.

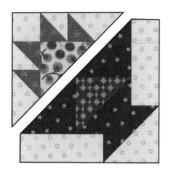

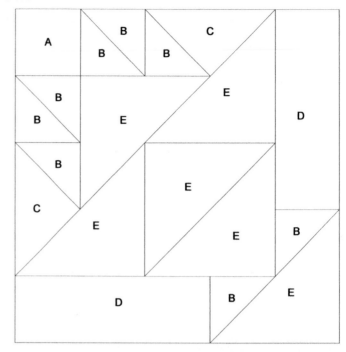

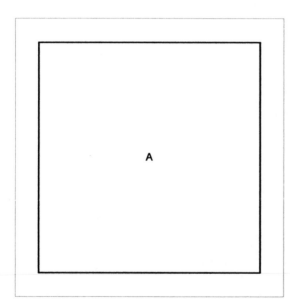

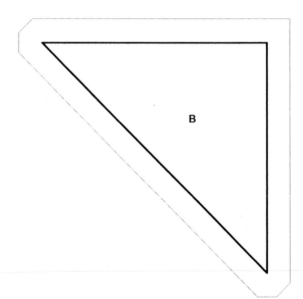

From The Kansas City Star, January 16, 1937: No. 486
Original size – 12"

This design was taken from a quilt made by Mrs. Mary Burr Cochran, widow of Andrew Cochran, in 1886, in Independence County, Arkansas. This pattern was contributed by Mrs. Carl A. Dumke, Bokoshe, Ok.

C

D

E

King's Crown

Appeared in The Star **April 11, 1931**

12" finished block

Fabric Needed
Red
Tan and red print
Green print

Cutting Instructions

From the red, cut
1 – 7 1/4" square. Cut the square from corner to corner twice on the diagonal or cut 4 triangles using template D.

From the tan/red print, cut
4 – 3 7/8" squares. Cut the squares from corner to corner once on the diagonal or cut 8 triangles using template B.
1 – 6 1/2" square (template C).
4 – 3 1/2" squares (template A).

To Make the Block

Sew a tan/red print B triangle to either side of a red D triangle as shown. Make 4.

Sew a green A square to each end of a B/D unit as shown. Make 2 rows like this.

Sew a B/D unit to either side of the C square as shown to make the center of the block.

Sew the three rows together as shown to complete the block.

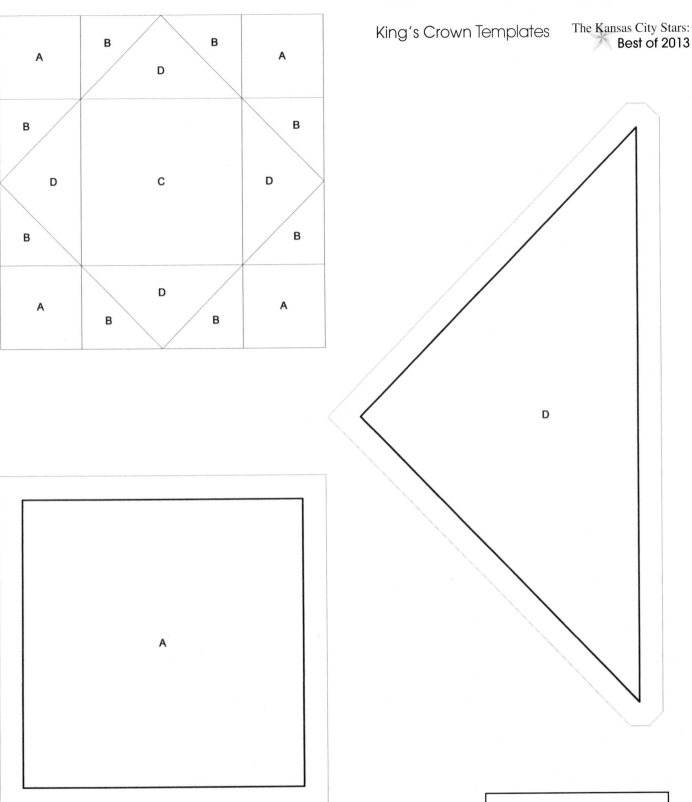

From The Kansas City Star, April 11, 1931: No. 165
Original size – 8 1/2"

After all, little girls are much the same as they were in their great-grandmother's time, for this nice quilt block comes from a little girl only 8 years old, who designed it herself and calls it "The King's Crown." She is Jean Spring, who lives on a farm near Bertrand, Neb. The block is nicely proportioned and other little girls would not find it hard to piece. Either plain or figured fabric may be used. Each one of the blocks may be different, which will make it more interesting to little folks. Plain blocks of the same size, 8-1/2 inches, may be used between the pieced ones. Allow for seams, and piece the block in rows.

B

C

Farmer's Daughter

Appeared in The Star **March 16, 1935**

Cutting Instructions

From the red fabric, cut

5 – 2 1/2" squares or use template A.

4 – 2 7/8" squares. Cut each square from corner to corner once on the diagonal or cut 8 triangles using template B.

From the green fabric, cut

8 – 2 1/2" squares or use template A.

4 – 2 7/8" squares. Cut each square from corner to corner once on the diagonal or cut 8 triangles using template B.

From the tan fabric, cut

4 – 2 1/2" squares or use template A.

Note: I changed this pattern so it would be easier to piece. The overall appearance is the same but there are no set-in seams.

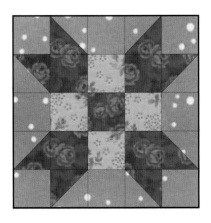

10" finished block

Fabric Needed
Red
Tan
Green

To Make the Block

Sew a green B triangle to a red B triangle to make a half-square triangle unit. Make 8.

Sew the squares and half-square triangles into 5 rows as shown below.

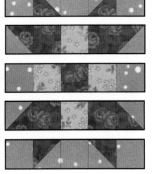

Sew the rows together to complete the block.

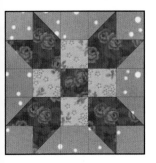

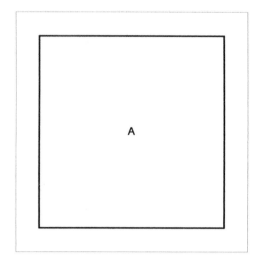

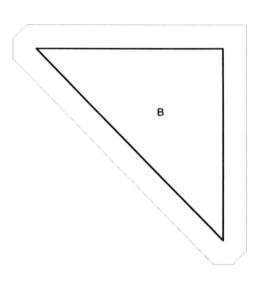

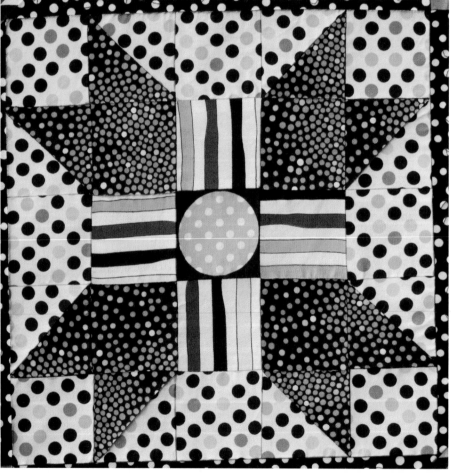

"Log Cabin for a Farmer's Daughter" by Sharon Wasteney, Hannibal, Mo.

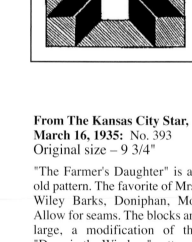

From The Kansas City Star, March 16, 1935: No. 393 Original size – 9 3/4"

"The Farmer's Daughter" is an old pattern. The favorite of Mrs. Wiley Barks, Doniphan, Mo. Allow for seams. The blocks are large, a modification of the "Dove in the Window" pattern.

"Log Cabin for a Farmer's Daughter,"
designed, pieced, and quilted by
Sharon Wasteney, Hannibal, Mo.